POETRY RIVALS 2012

A MOMENT OF STASIS

Edited by Helen Davies

First published in Great Britain in 2013 by:
Forward Poetry
Remus House
Coltsfoot Drive
Peterborough
PE2 9BF
Telephone: 01733 890099
Website: www.forwardpoetry.co.uk

Printed and bound in the UK by BookPrintingUK
Website: www.bookprintinguk.com

FOREWORD

In 2009, Poetry Rivals was launched. It was one of the biggest and most prestigious competitions ever held by Forward Poetry. Due to the popularity and success of this talent contest like no other, we have taken Poetry Rivals into 2012, where it has proven to be even bigger and better than previous years.

Poets of all ages and from all corners of the globe were invited to write a poem that showed true creative talent - a poem that would stand out from the rest.

We are proud to present the resulting anthology, an inspiring collection of verse carefully selected by our team of editors. Reflecting the vibrancy of the modern poetic world, it is brimming with imagination and diversity.

As well as encouraging creative expression, Poetry Rivals has also given writers a vital opportunity to showcase their work to the public, thus providing it with the wider audience it so richly deserves.

CONTENTS

THE POEMS

A ROYAL SALUTATION BY A LOYAL MEMBER OF THE NATION
(To HM EIIR, 1952-2002-2012)

Harken – echoes come this way
Of the pageant of the day
Of procession strangely strayed
From the city to the glade,
Lining lanes, each glowing flower
Joins to celebrate the hour.
Buttercups, with hoards untold,
Shining cloth-of-gold unfold;
Forget-me-nots and Campions,
And Stitchworts are companions
In the nation's colours true,
Flags and bunting red, white, blue;
Hedgerows fringed with Queen Anne's lace
Fit to frame a royal face.
Foxgloves chimes and changes ring,
Bluebells tinkle ting-a-ling.
Bishop ferns their crosiers raise
In a pastoral hymn of praise.
Lords-and-Ladies proudly wait
Representing pomp and state;
Rose and Woodbine scramble high
All the better to espy.
Even Primrose lingers on,
Pale, though, with strength nearly gone.
All unite in rural scene
The celebration of our Queen.

N D Wood

IT'S JUST BIOLOGY

Having a baby is nothing special.
It's nothing exciting.
No big deal.
It's just a series of compositions in chemistry.
Everybody does it. It's just how it's meant to be.
It's easy.
It's expected.
It's just so elementary.
It's just biology, he said to me.
. . . He had the cheek to state to me.
He felt the need berating me.
Enraging me.
But the truth is more than you can know, my friend.
The job may begin but it sure never ends.

Because,
To grow that life inside of you,
Belonging to you
And be one with you.
Then split –
Into two.
And expel into the world,
So suddenly.
So violently.
And yet so planned and mindfully.
(Shoot that hurts)
And to cherish them then,
So passionately.
Consumingly.
They are the stars and moon of me.
It's like,
You could burst at the seams,
Any moment it seems.
At the sheer unimagined gravity,
Of 'oh my!' what exactly,
Does it really mean?
To be their hopes and guide their dreams,
Until they themselves have learned and seen,
And for them to be –
So grown up . . .
It's everything and so much more.
It's worth a hundred times 'before'.
To hold so tight so preciously,
This wonder of necessity.

'To perpetuate the human race'.
The future of it all, held –
In such a tiny, perfect face.

I demand of you to think again,
Rearrange your thoughts and open up that brain.
Think once more on what it means,
To grow a life and set it free.
Do you have the capacity,
To understand the enormity,
Of bringing such a soul as this,
So pure as this,
So whole as this . . .
Who's yet to grow as much as this,
Into such a world . . .
As this?
Deformed conformity and fear to be.
Listen to my words and see,
And pray, think again dear friend.
Let your mind and ties that bind unbend.
And dare you try to tell me –
That it's nothing
But
Biology.

Molly Garner

MY SON

On the 22nd of March 1972 was the day you were born
When I held you in my arms you were so soft and so warm.
The happiness you brought to my life you will never know
I just wanted to tell you how I love you so.
The sadness and the laughter I have shared every minute
It has been a better world for having you in it.
Infant, junior and senior, the years have gone so fast
But the memories that are in my heart, they are the things that will last.
You have given so much pleasure to my life the laughter and so much fun
I am so very happy that I had you and so proud that you are my son.

Josephine Horsted

I AM NINETEEN YEARS OLD AND I THE DAY THE 'LECCY CAME BACK ON

'Touch me again and I'll stick this fork in your eye,'
The young boy was heard to cry
He'd just taken another beating for no reason
'Go on you fat cow! Take his side now,'
He'd scream out again, still in pain
She'd turn away, only herself to blame?
It wasn't a beating from thugs in the street
But from another drunken swine that she'd always meet
Who kept them in misery, never working a day?
Scraps were all that'd be left for them on the plate.

Just a few hours before it was all so nice
He'd saved their arses again when the police came
Knocking on the door, saying they'd had a complaint
They'd got the 'leccy back on again a neighbour said
And in a flash she denied it wasn't her fault
Pointed the finger at the boy and said,
'It was him, honest officer, we were cut off
But when I came back from the shop
He said he'd got it working, he can explain.'
All eyes turned and she said, 'Don't tell lies or cause us shame.'

So he had to lie to the cop; was lucky he was stupid
He knew him from the beat; it was hard on the streets
And when he didn't understand he said, 'Don't do it again lad
I'll let you off this time and caution Mum and Dad.'
Sure enough cut off again and that's when it started
The boy was blamed by him, but he wasn't the guilty party
And when he told them he wanted no more part of it
All the lies, cheatin' and stealin' that went on
Just another day, that's the breaks, no thanks
But here's a boot in the gut and a fist in your face
So you don't ever forget your place

That evening as he lay on his bed
His blood congealed on the pillow
He started to get ideas in his head
How he'd be better off dead
But as he listened to Jim's words
It came to him then, it would be the end
Not for him but them; If only he had a plan
He would surely do it but when?
Falling asleep as the music went on

In the morning he'd wake, the hate would be gone
Till next time it happens, he may go thru' with it
'Cause he can't take any more of this bullshit.

Bile suppressed, no one wills what they can't digest
It can only stay down a while
Until it comes back when you least expect
He decided time wasn't right, to put up a fight
So he started to write, put them all down with pen, not sword
And one day he'd strike when they let down their guard
It wouldn't be so hard, so he wrote down this word
Telling all what happened before, so one day
Everyone would know the score, and why he blew them away.

David McDonald

SLEEP WITH MICKEY MOUSE

But not in the sexy way, you crude thing . . .
I like teddy bears, you see.
Teddy bears are good for me.
They listen carefully to what I say.
They do not judge.
They cannot judge.
They cannot stare, or turn the other way.
They are good company, night and day.
No matter how old I get, or how young I act,
I can rely on my teddy bear pact.
They are friends, solace, nostalgia and fluff
in adorable shapes,
each and every one.
I love them all, down to the last stitch.
Even the faulty ones!
Though, if one spoke ill of me . . .
I might throw it at a wall, you see.
Or at least think about it . . .
Who would be there to ease the guilt, after all,
once I had thrown all of my teddy bears at the wall?

Katy Osborne

THIS IS NOT A PRISON

The screams and beef you hear as you walk in
The restless vibe and the unsettled grin

The alarms rain around the building
The offenders are batting with no fielding

The shift seems unending before it's began
The staff ordered to get the battering ram

The calm condemned wait around to see
The frightened searching for that non-existing glee

The crew take their stand at the enemy's door
The manic fella's ready to hit the floor

The bang and shouts as the staff ball through
The job's uneasy, this isn't a level two

The pile on begins with aggression at a high
The nurse getting ready to jab the thigh

The time goes on and energy wears thin
The troubled individual has no longer the grin

The team see the door and begin to move out
The restless now out cold and unable to shout

The sadly convicted can't help their mind tricks
The cells hold blame for most of the ticks

The staff lick their wounds and brag about power
The unnecessary victim feeling like a fallen tower

The mind is a limited thing with no control
The inmate will never have encouraged parole

The inmate in this case is a patient for sure
The wrecked mind will never see the front door

The prison is a mind game for all included
The prison is a mental hospital full and deluded

The abuse and alarms never leave this place
The hospital will never run a fair race.

Michael Hinton

UNCLE 'ERBERT

Has anybody seen my uncle 'Erbert?
He brought us to this seaside place so grand,
But my silly bruvver Neville,
The rotten little Devil,
Has buried Uncle 'Erbert in the sand.

The family has searched the beach for hours,
And we're worried, all except for Auntie Min,
She's a proper optimist,
And she stubbornly insists
That we're bound to find him when the tide comes in.

But it's getting late and turning rather chilly,
We've found the car, but no one can unlock it,
For 'Erb who had a cough,
Never took his jacket off,
And he's got the blinkin' car keys in his pocket.

The local lifeguard wasn't very helpful,
He just lay there on his towel getting browned,
He told us rather sadly
That he would have helped us gladly,
If only Uncle 'Erbert had got drowned.

It's a shame the day has ended in disaster,
For all the trouble Uncle 'Erbert took,
Now we're off to catch a train,
But we'll all come back again
Next weekend, and have another look.

Ron Missellbrook

SKINNY

She always sat on her own
That didn't matter; she was skinny
She never seemed quite at home
It didn't matter; she was skinny
Why did boys not turn her way?
I'm sure they did; she was skinny
She never needed them to stay
She had everything, and she was skinny

I saw how she scanned the place
Searching for another slender face
None of us were so high to reach her demands
None of us could begin to understand
What a joy to be so beautiful.

Her fingernails were peeling
That didn't matter; she was skinny
Her pointed nose was bleeding
It didn't matter; she was skinny
And she covered up her pale arms
Like she was ashamed to be so skinny
The bruises shone with broken harm
But they were perfect, as she was skinny

She told me how she lost her mind
And I thought, oh isn't she so kind
To share with me her advice and tips
The way to make a healthy girl sick
We too could be so beautiful

I found my bones in a heaving pit
Of misery and cold hard shit
The dirt caved in and I couldn't escape
And I needed another slender face
For only they could understand
What stakes this burden does demand

I could feel my skin begin to dry
It wouldn't matter if I was skinny
When I saw my reflection, I screamed at her
'Why can't you be skinny?'
My teeth were rotten, my hair grey
How was everyone else so skinny?
Now I needed to fade away
To be *more* than just skinny

And with my hands down my throat
The urged me to play the game
Funny how as I destroyed myself
They still didn't know my name
Of course I wanted attention
But I know that we all do
That doesn't mean I'm lying
Or that this couldn't happen to you

And she told me just how sorry she was
That I was trapped in this hell
She told me how she too
Didn't mean it, when she fell
From a time when she was beautiful

But let our screams go unheard
Too afraid to speak, too skinny
I want you to be *sick* of that word
And never again say skinny
It didn't show the way she cried
Why should she cry? She was skinny.
Or under her clothes, her suicide
She had everything, but she was skinny.

Ellen Taylor (17)

TO PORTSMOUTH

Like a huge hug you surrounded me
Like an old friend you made me feel well
Each corner, each street, each tree
Smiled at me and never I was alone or bad.

I left you, but with a promise
I'll come back and visit you
My new and old friend, too
Oh dear, keep your lively smile.

Maria Nicodemo

STEP BY STEP

Parched, weary and aching,
A young girl struggles,
A big burden balanced,
On the precipice
Of her delicate and fragile head.

Staggering,
One foot in front of the other,
Bare, scratched and toughened
By the soiled roots of the dry ground,
As she digs deep
Into her African roots
To honour her dependent family.

Six feet long was her burden,
Forcefully heavy
On her three-feet tall feeble frame,
Forced to grow stronger,
Calling to duty ever sinew.

Interwoven, her thoughts, feelings and aspirations,
Caught up
In the interlocking, stiff, hooking branches,
Broken, bound and tied.
Her tired, bruised body burned with pain,
For the fate of this fire wood,
Her view of the world
Disintegrating
Into ashes
With every step.

A cool, refreshing breeze,
Blowing through her hot microclimate,
The wind whispering words of encouragement.
Like oxygen to an ember,
Her dreams were rekindled.
The more she wandered through the endless possibilities,
Each step brought her closer
To her passion, her destiny,
Finally rediscovered,
Reignited.

Another stumble.
Back to reality.
Yet unforgettable were her dreams.

Step by step.
She may not be there now,
But one day
She will.

Andrew Steele

RAIN IS STEADY

Rain is steady
Rain arrives in an orderly manner
And rain can pace itself
Because rain has stamina
Rain doesn't deposit all at once
Because rain knows how to queue
So tell me
Why don't you?

Rain knows when to surge
And when to make a fuss
When to deluge
Like a panicked mob
So tell me,
Why do I have to teach you?

Rain can be rude
Rain jumps queues
Me, me, me raindrops
In a motorway pile up
But, sometimes, I long to be
The steel barrier you crashed into.

Rain can be late
Rain diverts
Rain delays
You know the rain

Even the rain knows
It must wait sometimes
Even the ocean knows
It cannot take up residence
In the whole of the sky

So tell me
Why do I have to teach you?

Chris Stewart

THE WATCHER

In search of something you could never name, the jaune of a smile or the blue of a glance, you are at the Censier Daubenton Station. Do you see that young girl wearing headphones, a dark blue jacket and a petrol scarf, la tête dans les nuages in these demented lands?
Well, that's you.

You have no idea why the station is called Censier Daubenton.
Never been curious. You think it's probably named after an old man who lived unhappy, surrounded by shadows.
The station is crowded, people rushing everywhere.
Names for nameless things.

You're in the metro. *Place Monge.* You can hear someone speaking in your headphones.
Who's that person telling you a story? *Jussieu. Sully Morland. Pont Marie.* It must be a man. He's telling you a story. He might be somewhere in the crowd, reading the story now.
He told you some nice stories and one not.

A lesson about falling. *Châtelet.* You try to pick him out from the crowd.
Is it that man over there, wearing glasses? He doesn't seem to look at you. Maybe the other one sitting next to him? Maybe not. Eventually he comes into view.
There are no boundaries.

I think you met some time ago, remember? He was walking on his side of the Earth, you were wandering around yours . . . You were so close you could count his eyelashes and almost touch his sharp teeth.
Slow motion.

You got closer and closer till your ribs intertwined themselves in a violent grip, his collarbone entered your chest and pierced your heart, and no one could tell for sure whose skin and eyes and bones and eyelashes and blood and teeth they were.
skineyesboneseyelashesbloodteethfracture

You can see your face mirrored in the window of another metro almost brushing against the one you're in. He talks to metro travellers around him, miming the mannerism of the lives he didn't get the chance to live. Clumsy hands, wobbly voice.
Weakness.

They don't know he's telling a story, they don't know about you two.
And you revel in this intimate act, as if you were his double. What do you see? A big forehead, a mouth. Then someone else's face.
His mouth again, his right hand, his eyes,
Then nothing.

There is some poetry in this tender curiosity.
In the thought of a metro in motion.
The thought of the thought of a metro in motion.
Pont Neuf.

Felicia Cucuta

TRANQUILLITY

I find You in a moment, unhurried, free from time,
In beauty and in stillness; unmarred yet unrefined,
Where nature meets creation, unspoilt and untamed,
You're there in all Your glory; unreligiously en-framed.

I savour each refreshing as I catch You in the breeze,
For You've hidden Heaven's echoes in the whisper of the trees.
You saturate the sky with a heavy sense of peace,
And the wispy clouds that paint it, bring soothing and release.

I try to think of nothing, but deftly, thoughts invade,
Yet here You've banned the dark ones and kindly they've obeyed.
A rest for weary minds; unladen; in respite,
Serenity brings hope; restores your jaded sight.

Light and shade find balance, with pleasure bound in each,
And as You seek to guide me, illustrate and teach,
I look at my life differently; discernment takes a view,
For it's not just in the sunshine, You nurture and renew.

The solace of a moment in a tranquil, hidden place,
Can multiply the healing of Your balm of love and grace.
A jot in time can flourish, evolve to something more,
As You give me strength to live and give me wings to soar.

From here I see such beauty: impressive, grand design,
Invented at the maker's wheel, and fused with power divine.
Each butterfly and flower, plant and tree and hill,
Narrates Your endless wonder, unmatched by human skill.

The facets of Your glory, reflect in what You've made,
There's harmony in colour, purpose in each shade.
There's wisdom in all movement; every form unique:
You're here concealed in everything, for those that choose to seek.

Where once we had an Eden; perfection, God with Man,
There now exists a void; a blemish in Your plan.
So You have scattered Eden, in seeds, throughout the Earth,
And here I think I'm resting . . . where a seed has given birth!

Juliet Dawn Doolan

CHAMPAGNE 'N' GUTTERS

Clutching the belongings of the brand new tramp,
like clasping constellations to keep warm on the tarmac road I stamp.
Watching the stars of Centauros a billion miles away
bleed to death as the train whistles through metal, garbage, onto the neon light of day,
the other millionaire tramps, fairy-tale forest beards, with shoes who beg retirement
they are wedding rings in mud, to get a few dollars by any means
'*Sale:* 20% discount on Plastic Futures, Wishes, and Unreachable Dreams!'
running my hands along the sands of Jupiter, while asteroids, graze my skin,
The towns and industries are littered as if they are wish lists of poems on a bedroom floor
and all this lonesome long time I wish I could wish for more.

The car like me falls breathless like a dying dog, weeping its guts and angry passenger,
selling it now, $200 from a pair of yellow teeth behind a counter.
I choose a bar like a thief chooses a pocket
Now I'm stuck tonight, as an insect caught in a sticky drop of petrol
I try to find a light to write and read, yet also remember I don't have a place to sleep.
Roaches. As many as there are televisions in the West.
Life is as unbearable as a concrete mattress, or no food, or no guests.
All this time I remember the taste of champagne and the stench of the gutter I have made my damp cot
an advert for 'James' Ready-Made Meals' as a pillow, but its paper starts to rot.

Cleveland – Chicago – Cheyenne.
Cops on my filthy tail.
The trip gets as barmy as my handwriting
I'll settle for the furthest of places,
San Francisco?
(Flower bracelets wrapped around a beer bottle),
or Vegas
(Roulette wheels rotating for a new life.)
Now I just watch TV in a motel room,
I imitate a rich man, but stop when my rags get caught on the 'budget bought' 'superstore sale' bed
Words and phrases creep from under rocks and verandas at my call as whiptail lizards
I'm inspired, as I reach for a pen; my head fills with ink to write and explodes wit jealous thought
my arms are thinner than sympathy, I wish they were not mine,
Dear Diary, distance – I'm finally dreaming from a dirty cardboard sign.

Today I'm hitchhiking.
walking up the highway with a baked bean can
thumb out like a lopsided telegraph pole –
I say a destination, but they're only going as far as Salt Lake, maybe you know it, that plain of solitary water
they give me some advice but it's gone. I hope I can ring their twenty-something daughter.
Along the road, the other hobos appear, all hogging the verge like rogue ants on buffalo meat,

I'm slowly replacing perfume and marble with cheap paint and blistered feet.
I meet Jim Bridger Mountain Man on the highway, fur around his neck and gun for trapping,
he gives me directions for dreaming losers who wish for untroubled napping.

Food: Check, (but limited)
Frustration: In Excess
I need to raise money for the next worn-out leg,
so I've started with a few beer cans and a plastic bag from cheap supermarkets
and the map's veins and arteries spread to mock unkempt ivy on an English cottage.
The road bends and flexes like a spin over cranked metal, grinding at a steady rate,
Leaving a full stop, a poem, a kiss, and some urine on the soft body of every graceful state.

James Gemmill

WOMAN ON THE CANAL BOAT

I do not know you
You come and sit at my table
You say a cancellation has occurred.
You sit and you are silent.

The boat moves off, it is filled with a bunch of varied folk.
The couple opposite speak to me about their many trips.
She is oriental, he is English
A varied cross section of folk wonderful.
I listen into their conversations, I people-watch too.

I walk to the front and watch as we move through the locks.
The woman follows and stands next to me
She speaks about herself and why she is here,
I respond with a similar conversation
We become friends.

Rosemarie Kraftchenko

FLAMENCO DANCER IN PECKHAM

She opens blinking eyes and
paints patterns on the ceiling
with her gaze and index finger
and she doesn't want to move.
His arm rests on her chest and although she is a dancer
this confinement is entrancing –
a solitary wonder
under bed sheets from Ikea.
The polyester threads recording memories
in her head that she hopes will be
an entry in a catalogue of times like this.

He doesn't stir.
Suddenly she's planning holidays
to Italy and Spain
the insane part of her thinking he'll abstain from any other
now they've watched that film and eaten food you eat
when you're trying not to fall in love.

Dust floats in the sunlight.
She marvels at how skin
that was so alive
eight hours ago
can show no sign of the delight
induced by wine and conversation.

Now she wants to be up.
To lose herself in cups of coffee
and lazy Sunday mornings.
Meeting people on park benches
like you do in play rehearsals
and she wants to do all of this with him.

She wants to make new memories
because the old ones
are growing rusty,
like wheel rims on a bicycle
you haven't ridden in a while
that turn and creak inside you head,
leaving flakes of what you've lost.

He wakes.

She loses her smile because she's gotten carried away again
and men before couldn't recall her name and
what if he asks her to leave and she's left
to weave her aspirations with harsh reality

and see that what you wish for really doesn't come –
'Hi,'
he whispers.
Their eyes lock intermittently
until his stomach rumbles.
His laughter is beautiful and resonating
and he's deliberating over which
coffee shop they should go to.
One serves freshly-squeezed orange juice,
the other plays flamenco music.
'It doesn't matter,' he says,
'we can go to the other one next time.'
She finds her voice
after swallowing the lump held in her throat.
Her feet are tapping.
She becomes a flamenco dancer in Peckham;
he beckons her with the only bit of information she wants to hear, right now.

Elisha Owen

CULTURE

Let's demonise the poor, a popular culture
Its essence of insidious dealings.
A politician shouts on a soap box of choice,
These people are the scourge of mankind,
They rob and cheat, as well as being benefit cheats.
A tabloid the politician message.
The hurt and pain these words of choice,
Our a collective of people in high places.
The revelation is a collection of decades,
Where people are still suffering in silence.
Where politicians should help with
Privilege and privy but don't for their own salvation.
Time and time as decades come and go
The fabric of the political system is failing.
Its people and bankers entourage it covers,
It's broken, broken, broken.

Gary Summers

SHE CAME UNAWARES

love, love, love
and children just happen
likewise in the same disguise
she came into my life
took my breath away
captured my heart forever
made me slog day after day
in her sweet little breaths when asleep
my heart dived and rejoiced into oceans deep;
am I a mother or a lover?
you couldn't tell
this is love, the incomprehensible love
that knows no bounds
goes same way for the lover, rings the bell
and comes rebound!
Nearly ten years old
has hooked my heart and given me a bond stronger than gold
if I were to be blessed with powers of God
there're only few things that I would plod
fulfill her life with the happiness cake
which for her would be a game of give and take!
A star that she has turned out this far
may she keep her magic alive and continue her hard work
so that opportunities at every step wait for her ajar!
I bless her always and wish her the best
is it possible to put a mother's heart to a test?
she has made me vulnerable to the point of a break
the very bond that gives me equal strength to put anything at stake!
I can go on writing forever for her
as this love knows no bends
but realise it's a poem for Poetry Rivals
and so, thanking y'all, here it ends.

Ripple Gupta

STAY AWAY

I told you to stay away
To stay away, stay away
But my message got too vague
It went to Venice, to Prague
You retorted with a slur
Said my features made a blur

I shouted from my deep lung:
Keep away, you're slimy dung
Just stay away, stay away
But then you just had to stay
Said I sounded rather vague
You disgust me, take the cake

So stay away, stay away
Don't make my day look dull grey.

Muhammad Khurram Salim

MY DAD

You took my hand
And guided me through
I just do not know
What I'll do without you

I close my eyes
And take a big sigh
Then I raise my head
And look up to the sky.

You're not here anymore
But what can I do?
All that I know
Is I love and miss you.

Toni Rhodes

MANY SPOKES TO THIS BIKE

Hail the young executive with his cycling clips and good looks.
Lavish tailored suits and a leather case; fine fashions scream at the chase.
His style ill suits pedaling in this race but all girls swoon at that well groomed face.
Hail the City as lively as it is vain.

Hail the socialite with her retro French bike and her positive posture.
Summer clothes accentuate her form but her bare arms bristle in the breeze.
She turns heads as she passes like a brief flash of summer sunshine amid the gloom.
Hail the beauty of youth.

Hail the mature enthusiast clad in his cycling bodysuit garb.
Advancing years belay hidden strength beneath that polymer skin . . .
But do reveal an expanding girth that defies any rational fashion selection.
Hail those older but no less wise.

Hail the career girl with her laptop hid in leather and a brolly in her basket.
Practicality and professionalism marry with perfect riding skills . . . and angry haste.
This lady knows where she wants to be and the road there is merely a metaphor.
Hail the ambitious for they strive while others sloth.

Lest we forget the tribe of couriers with their dreadlocks and tats.
Symbiotically attached to their dirtied bikes with screaming radios and low slung sacks.
Sinews like steel match the frames of their transport.
Hail the free for they are no less trapped.

The light is red; we must wait as the city's traffic ebbs and flows.
A rash young man defies the law and hurtles over the abandoned box junction.
'Tut tut young man,' we do not hail you.
We do not hail you!

I arrange the pedal with my best foot first, and watch the lights. I'm ready for the off.
The exec taps an iPhone, the enthusiast adjusts his clinging credentials and the model flicks her hair.
Motionless the courier balances, poised like a ballerina, to spite gravity. We wait.
Hail diversity, it is our strength.

No pithy salute to my kind; that seems a tad unfair. I'm the odd one here, not these others.
A mid-range commuter on a rental bike from barmy Boris, our unique mayor.
I wear the wrong clothes and my lack of fitness cakes me in sweat.
You have my sympathy Mr Johnson.
'He who is tired of London is tired of life,' a wise man once said
Hail London.

Richard Lowe

FOR ALL

A loving abandonment, freedom of choice,
Words pour out, wired together, volunteered,
Throw letters against the wall, to see what sticks
Reaction, reacting, beautify vulgar images,
Articulate your love, a passionate revolt,
Answers seem lost to all, oblivious, distorted,
Deceptive, a labyrinth of lies,
The human menagerie, caged for your pleasure,
Hack away endlessly, anonymous, evokes all,
Occupy your will, knowledge is power,
Dissect everything, magnify your mind,
God's vomit tasted sour,
Drowned in an immaculate lust,
Have no fear, we'll organise your soul,
We'll dominate your pleasure and your pain,
Description of thoughts, a positive approach,
Bar the code that screams red,
An individual coma, a surrogate being.
It's a blessing and a curse,
The mundane enveloping everything.

Brian Barnwell

TWINKLE, GLITTER, GLISTEN

You touched my soul
As you stepped within
Your voice so insatiable
I couldn't sleep.

That split second look
What does it mean?
My attraction to you
Unexplained.

I feel so at peace
Kiss me deep, strip me
Naked and consume me
Whole.

Sacha Sandon

UNTITLED

It's Rebecca's first day at a new school and she's nervous.
Heart pacing, mind racing but keeping calm on the surface.
See at her old school she worked hard but seldom got a mention
So here's a fresh start to finally gain some attention.
First lesson she arrives early and sits at the back of the class,
Until some other kids come in and tell her to move her arse.
'These sets are reserved for those that don't want to be observed'
She's hurt but gets up and moves without saying a . . .
Come break time she stands alone in the sunshine
And all she ever wanted was some time in the limelight
That night, she makes a promise as she cries herself to sleep,
That when the sun rises she'll find some company to keep.
Now it's the fourth day, third lesson and she's sick of being seen through,
Having no one to talk to, let alone cling to.
Rationalises to herself that she has nothing to lose
And that to pay her dues means she has to break the rules.
See, Rebecca's eyes always seem to focus on the kids who don't focus.
Who mess about in class and whose schoolwork goes unnoticed.
And to fit in with them, their peer pressure will help shape you,
Mould you into someone even you can't relate to.
So she begins to go through little episodes,
Has letters sent home, parents blame it on puberty and pheromones.
See Daddy can't digest that his little princess
Is starting to keep her cards close to her chest.
Her grades begin to slip which she didn't intend
Cigarettes are two'sed up behind the bike sheds.
After school, come nightfall, find her drinking on a park bench,
She finds her confidence by running in a pack of false friends.
Rebecca knows better, but that doesn't matter,
This is the right here and now, and she wants a piece of the action.
Soon she becomes the talk of the town, the talk of the staff room,
Yeah that girl who gave off such a good first impression
Is now at the heart of every lesson, she can barely keep attention.
Excels in profanity with her excellent vocabulary
And even when the teacher's words are potent
Rebecca's still an addict to her BlackBerry.
Top of the class in forgetting homework, to her school's a joke,
Nothing but an attitude, short temper and a short skirt.
This carries on for a couple of years,
And her parents gradually learn their worst fears.
But after the repeated arguments, broken plates and shattered glasses,
They reassure each other it is just a phase, and when Rebecca gets in late
They stop pestering her for answers.
And then one night there comes a knock at the door.

Mum goes and opens it and is scared at what she sees.
Rebecca quickly runs upstairs,
Leaving Mum to call Dad and together they stand hand in hand,
Listening to the words spoken from a policeman.
'Broke into her school, criminal damage, arson
Headmaster has no choice, hands are tied, expulsion.'
The policeman leaves and they begin their discussion
What' the remedy for this concoction? What should be her punishment?
They go upstairs and enter Rebecca's bedroom,
She's got her duvet pulled tight over her head,
It's what she used to do to keep safe from the monsters under the bed.
Dad has second thoughts and taps Mum's arm, beckoning towards the door,
Mum frowns but gives in, 'Let her think about what she's done to them.'
A week later and it's Rebecca's first day at a new school and she's nervous.
Heart pacing, mind racing but keeping calm on the surface.
She has a second chance to start again and make amends,
But I still don't know how her story will end.

Jack Wells

THE CLOCK - A BALLAD OF TIME

You stand with grace and graven face
Eternal and sublime,
And hour by hour your hands devour
Our lives, our loves, our time.

Upon dark wings the raven sings
Laments of time you toll,
And thus your chime, that ancient rime,
Still holds Man's heart and soul.

The moon and stars, a thousand scars,
Your fingers trace their path;
Time falls in sands to bony hands
In love, in pain, in wrath.

The layers of dust, the rasp of rust,
Your key does nature turn;
And yet, tick-tock, still breathes the clock
While dreams of youth you burn.

Michelle Scott

EXTRAORDINARY

When he smiles,
it's like opening your eyes underwater:
seeing a new world
through a new pair of eyes.
It's like he paints the world
a brand new colour,
made up of the purest
and brightest light until
the Shadows and the Darkness
run to the furthest corner of
the galaxy.

I wish I could take his smile
and paint my house that colour.
I could pain a thousand canvases
that are more beautiful than
Da Vinci, Debussy, and God's fingerprint.
I wish to add this colour
to my Dulux chart.
I wish to name it
Extraordinary.

Rachel Glass

EARTH CRIES

We drill her for oil.
We mine her for coal.
We pollute her with poisons.
We dig her for gold.
No wonder the Earth screams!

Rachel Hobson

DRESS TO IMPRESS

This dress hates me.
Linings, layers, I am lost.
It is like wearing the entire contents of Fabricland,
I am drowning in a glowy, cloudy, taffeta world,
where cotton candy and tissue paper are king
and any hint of rebellion is quashed under another layer of scratchy gauze.
I am a twenty-year-old girl in a five-year-old's dress.
An ugly sister in Cinderella's ballgown, a shrimp in a Quality Street wrapper
A radiant tiara on the head of a donkey.
A hippo in a ballerina's tutu, an empty crisp packet in a coy pond,
I am red wine on a wedding dress, a dirty mark on a fresh white sheet.

I am suffocating, the whale's bones want revenge.
A malicious malaise,
I can never live up to the expectations of this dress.
It deserves to be admired, to be followed with fury,
To draw envious looks from petulant girls
a romantic fantasy in waves of silk.

My glamorous nemesis.
On the hanger it is limp and innocent.
But on the mannequin it is alive,
its own fabulous being,
it drapes and hangs like a frozen waterfall,
one that shifts in the breeze.
It is far more beautiful than me.

So I told it to get stuffed and wore a skirt instead.

Annie Cash

AH, IGNORANCE

Ignorance is confident,
and strong and brash and bold.
Ignorance knows nothing else,
and he will not be told.

Ignorance, ah Ignorance,
you're certainly a card!
Many a wrong or stubborn view,
because of you, dies hard.

A misguider of the masses!
You're certainly one of these.
They begin to see the proverbial woods –
so you remind them of the trees.

'His Royal Denseness' subjects crow,
your clouded empire expands.
It is your will how much they learn –
playing right into your hands.

The masses are surely ignorant,
you've a real vice grip on they,
but your job is far from finished,
whilst Knowledge is at play.

Your age-old nemesis, Knowledge,
with his thirst for wisdom so,
he has proven quite infallible –
a learned man's hero.

Despite the power Knowledge has,
his humility is blatant,
unlike you, Ignorance; naturally,
you're arrogant and flagrant.

For Knowledge knows, naturally,
he's yet to know it all,
whilst Ignorance, who thinks he does,
is destined for a fall.

Ignorance is ignorant,
and ignorant of this!
If he only knew, what he knew not,
he'd know he was not Bliss.

For Ignorance, is only Bliss,
to a fool, with far to go.
But Ignorance is a fool himself,
so I guess he would not know.

Tarik Ross-Cameron

WORLDLY SAVAGES: DANCE

I trace the concrete streets that call most evenings.
In search of something;
lost to me. In hunger, I prowl and prance
for soul and sex and beats,
instinct
howling,
muffled, but I listen.

Follow the night. Through amber light, past 3am fights
descending down those drunken heights that dare
you eternally forward.
Stagger and stumble, towards the inevitable morning that will follow:
the bruise and bite of your misspent, weekend night,
searching for soul in a cider can.

And no one goes to a nightclub for 'fun'.
Just like no one drinks a triple rum to 'relax' . . .

But an innate melody will always lead me back,
to the caverns of that club, like a sonic moth.
To the beat. To the beat. To the beat.
The burrowing bass that burns rhythm into backbone.
Dubstep parting, Dubstep pulsing, wombing, throbbing, growling within this cave,
Is what I seek for, here?
Buried beneath the blur?

Christopher Fear

A CYNIC'S PERSPECTIVE

I blame 'the Owl and the Pussycat'
For my high expectations of men.
He is rich, he's a hoot,
A musician to boot,
A dab wing with an oar – he's a ten.

He tempted her taste buds with honey
And he tickled her whiskers with prose.
For a year and a day
He did not fly away –
Then was bird-brained enough to propose!

So it seems like a fairy-tale ending
As they dance in the silver moonlight
But I've got a cat
I know better than that
No; something does not add up right.

Cats flirt with the birds in the winter
They invite them for tea in the spring
When they cannot escape
It's a marvellous jape
To play with their entrails like string.

So forgive me for being a cynic
But this marriage is not worth a fig.
Now the Owl, he's just swell
But, my friends, I can tell
That the Cat had her eye on the Pig.

Stacy Stroud

ALONG THE WATERWAYS

Along the waterways we ride,
There since time immortal.
Built by Man, and shaped by nature,
All with a sense of pride.

Once upon a time, the factories used to thrive.
But all that has now changed,
Most of the factories that once stood tall,
Are either closed and bare,
Boarded up, to be locked away,
Haunting the waterways,
Others becoming open shells,
And piles of mass rubble,
Are all that's left of the buildings' remains,
Along with the spirit of the workers and their machines.
As the last of the factories barely survive.

What changes there have been.
The barges replacing horses,
Designer apartments replacing factories,
Day-tripping tourists replacing workers,
The old ways are no more.
These sights, no longer recognised,
With the workers disappearing,
And the closed factories pulled down,
Leaving just the rubble and destruction,
And a bare landscape that only the imagination can fill.
What stories these waters could tell,
If the workers could still be seen at their machines.

David Blakemore

BUDDLEIA

I open the cabinet
Losing my way
In a labyrinth of flowers
Following Alice
Again.

A flock of clouds swamping,
A few dots of the sky
Tries to rain,

An obscure light
Icing on the halos of spring onion shoots,
A few sooty tea bags
Flaking slowly like a sandstone
Façade;

So, here I am,
Tossing beneath a featherlike foliage,
When the last trail of a slug
Coughs through the mud.

Argus gargles
In a world of looking glasses,
Watching bumblebees
In his own eyes,
Licking the pollens on every mirror,
Counting his first
Pancreas
To the very hundredth,

Soon, every palate of appetites
multiply by number;

On the soaring wooden fence,
Reflect a hundred watching busts
Of a same entrepreneur,
Bodged on heaping bottles of Metformin
Tablets,

A million galaxies jarred by a same lauding pure white,
Holy, or sacrilegious,
Canonised as bubbly
As another million frilling foams of starched ruffs
On every early modern shift,

This season's prescription
Taunting before my face,
A world of aromatic sage

Agonising in the scents
Of a hundred wanton tongues
Sampling, relishing
Before guzzling down every tinge of sweetness
In the light of my eyes.

David Lin

IMPACT

Drink and drugs are as bad as each other,
Do you think taking them will make you stronger?
Well you're wrong, they won't.
They'll only make you weaker.

The excitement, the laughter, it may give you a thrill,
But the bad side to this, is that it can kill.
If you got hurt, then how would you feel?

Under the influence of drink and drugs,
Driving down the road – what a mug!
You don't know what you're doing and lose control
The car does a flip and then a roll.

Into a family car you fly
It's obvious they're all going to die.

You don't get off lightly, not at all,
Because what you have done is so damn cruel.
Skull cracked open, blood on the floor
Twisted leg in a twisted door.

With your head through the window
And your face torn apart,
Now there's no beat left in your heart.

Carys Kitchin

A MALE THONG
(Ode to middle-aged spread)

Should I put this to verse
Or maybe to song
About an old man who put on a thong.

To start at the back
That leads to the crack
Not a wrinkle in sight
There's nothing to hide
All is in line
There's nothing to mind

Then moving forward
To the case of the sack
Where the vegetables
Are clearly not laid on a rack

I think that for Christmas
I might get him a rack
And have it delivered
In Santa's red sack!

Then to the front
And what do we find?
All the fat
That's come from behind!

Now as I poise with my pen
Should I continue to write
Of a belly that clearly
Behaves like a jelly.

No this verse is unkind
I must clear out my mind
This verse has been fun
But the writing's now done.

Sue Weston

MY SKIN

My skin masks my true self within
Peppered face
Can this be me?

I'm a dark nun, solemn and silent
Head bowed low
So none will know

This ravaged rind causes recoil
With scars so deep
No creams will cure

This awkward gift puberty bore
For years I've worn
My loathsome suit

But the sun beams short-lived relief
The body tans
All sanded smooth

And I creep from my stubborn shell
To feel the warmth
Bathe my neck

Still perfect glass makes me retreat
All flaws exposed
My armour cracked

This pre-aged skin seals me inside
My truth I'll hide
Till healing comes

And I will look, look to the day
Blemishes fade
And fears dissolve

And new fruit will be revealed
I will stand tall
With peacock's pride

Fabia Turner

YELLOW BOAT
(Inspired by a glass picture by Kim Schofield)

Water calm,
As the Twenty-Third Psalm
Yellow boat
Floats
In Poole Harbour –
Bobbing gently
White foam
Like bubble-bath
Nudges
Against the blue hull –
A shrill, shriek of a gull.
Fish hide
From the lone angler on the quay,
Just a hint of a busy, buzzing bee
Sky blue,
Passing clouds
And in spite of the birds and the bees
There's a kind of peace.

Roy Goucher

UNTITLED

In part, this is what I see,
A requisite rhyme riddled in time;
Woven with the rigors of all that is mind

Once more, the tri-mast of the Silver Galleon
Ripples, each, with gold less molten
Sails made of birthing stars.
Held of Cedar petrified
In pendulous silvery motion
– Of which we glide,
Submerged,
High amongst Heaven's Tsars

Blown, 'shattered', on endless oceans.

John Michael Mullen

LIFTING THE MASK

Fake smiles and crocodile tears,
Laughing at all our deepest fears.

Disguising the people we really are,
No changing now, it's got us this far.

Hiding away,
No shouting out.

Afraid of being different,
Scared to stand out.

A slave to the rhythm,
Just one of the sheep.

Take off the mask,
For once be unique!

Mark Matthews

SOMEONE'S ANGEL

On the edge I stand teetering for an
adrenaline ride with no wings to glide.
Will an angel save me as I fall from
grace or is it my own demise? Am I just
an emotional disgrace with no right to be
saved? I do not often pray yet have hope, is
that close to faith? Does my soul, if I have
one, deserve an angelic hand? I awaken by a
tranquil river, on smooth cobbles I lay, which
seem to have broken my fall and clutching a
single white feather. At that waking moment
my mind is settled and open to all possibilities.

Andrew Craig

ROYALITY TV

'Don't Tell the Bride' is a programme on BBC Three
and, ultimately, it means very little to me besides
my licence fee and their episodic ten grand budget
to get married as the groom decides, and his bride
invariably hates it anyway, and him too by the end;
it is all just pretend, reality TV, how else could it be?
You don't usually defecate onscreen to strains of Coldplay
whilst just next door strangers debate your face,
but you're not royalty, are you?

But Prince William is, and his business is ours,
wiped and smeared all over the front pages
so that you can almost smell it; it is instinct
to steal a headline when passing a paper,
we are all news hounds, hungering for gossip,
for words to fill our vacuous days for the price
of a paper, or broadband, or the TV Licence,
longing to make the news, to be centre-stage,
but you're not royalty, are you?

It is an impossibility, like papal infallibility,
but when a prince drops to one knee, and proposes
everyone knows with upturned noses, it is big business
we're British, don't you know and we still salute
our royal family as it grows, and as Prince Philip goes
and calls another pauper a racist slur, we stand up
to sing 'God Save The Queen' together, selling papers,
sloshing our tea about, talking of greatness,
everybody wants to be famous,

and we still dream of empire on this tiny island,
but our spires have fallen, and we are insane,
and out of our pockets, our money is taken
to pay out for follies, and for polishing gold
and for royal weddings, for some untold 'joy'
and you do get a day off (if you work in a bank),
so be thankful for that; scrape, and bow down
to those Germans with their heads on our stamps,
we're not royalty, are we?

David Sealey

MY HERO

Steve
Steve
Steve

When I woke up I could not believe
That your life had been sucked away
By a giant southern stingray

When I was growing up as a boy
My life was on zero
Till I discovered Steve Irwin
And he was my hero
He'd fight with crocodiles
Kick them in the teeth
Fight with large sharks
In the Barrier Reef

Now you had a wife
And you had a baby
Your life was not boring
But bizarre and crazy
Snakes spat in your face
You were no fake
You lived for the danger
Because you liked the taste

Well I loved you on TV
And at the cinema I was a punter
When I saw you in that movie
The Crocodile Hunter
Well it was so much better
Than Hulk and Rocky 3
You were a loser to some
But a hero to me

Now you died twice
Came back to life
Could have given sight back
To the three blind mice
Now this is a poem
For you Steve from me
I hope they love you in Heaven
So RIP

Steve, Steve, Steve.

Wesley James Byrne

I AM

I am of the soil; the peat bogs made me:
sodden, clung with plant matter, crowned
with leaves and mewling-born-in smoke
conceived and in pungent smoke preserved;
this tan hide, this stretched leather coat
worn by these bleached bones, as they break
the coiled-spring colt of the seasons
to ride with the tribe of all that has died.

I am pulled from my mother, blood-pelted
and birth-slicked with estuarine mud;
the drowning gurgle of my first spat breath
begat the mighty tidal bore of newborn days,
and the sputtering start of this mammalian heart
felt the lost wings flutter and the tail flock free;
I am a writhing creature – both great and small
brethren of the grub, the polecat and the shrew.

I am formed of thick clay beds
strung under the deepest foundations;
I am scooped from the earth and remoulded
into vessels and pots, soon broken and buried;
and each hand turned, all lips touched
remain impressed in the damp clag –
these moments mark the mud flats of time
like a family walk captured in footprints . . .

I am the pebble shift and the wave's hiss,
sand bars and breakers defend my borders;
I squall across deserted sands and huddle
with the windswept colonists, in haven
of a journey's lull – a prayer of puffins full
moves me, as should a shrieking psalm of life:
all born and braved ere are of the brood – rejoice,
rejoice, for it is so!

I am the tick of antler pick on stone
and the hollow echo following the seams
down to a bone hoard – bison, deer and boy
burnt, gnawed, discarded and sluiced by
rich rains; I am any scrawl of paint on any
wall – a tag or daub, a sign or signal for
devotions, or a meal – a spear or shield;
the inside of my skull is still a painted cave.

I am the bend of rock and the gaping gorge,
I am the molten surge and a glacial creep,
I've seared myself into the blue iron ore, then
mined treasuries from the beds of silver and tin;
through stone I slip, leaving shining strips
ripe for dreams of furnace and factory:
a crown-stone to be, or a chieftain's torque
twisted; some spoons or a fine toothed drill-bit.

I am dusted with the chalk of the downs,
peppered with the seasonings of passing-by
as the grinding wind mills away, piece by piece,
all grist to the whirlwind thrown, and some of me
reseeded where I touch down – my soluble soul
finds groundwater, passed through bedrock, slides
along fissures and re-springs where the hills rise
up, to be a fountain of faith in a once-dry vale.

I am the heath, the moor and the tarn,
the blank slate lake and the steel sky stay
inked together in my eyes – I play with the kit
if creation and rid with the fallen meteor of
morning. I am the squealings of surprise
at death's sudden slit; and the smog from coal
burning fires of desire shall not erase me –
I am the spark that slings to Earth; one who knows
the universe is empty, but for all of us.

Paul Findlay

GLASS DRY

You look at me that way
Begging for me to need you
Why?
Can you not see I do not need you anymore?
I have put you down and have not been near you,
But still you persist to look at me
Tempting me, wanting me,
Waiting for that excuse to lead me back to you.
The bottle is half-empty
But the glass is dry.

Lorraine Welch

THE SEAGULL AND THE SNACK

To understand my tale,
there is something you should know,
as far as you may travel,
as wide as your horizons grow,
you will never meet another,
with a love so pure and true,
for sweet, chocolate or pastry,
and no fear of this love to let it show.

I was sitting by the pier,
bathing in the sun,
not entirely sober,
and having great fun,
water beneath my feet,
the clearest I had ever seen,
I saw all the life beneath,
on the surface, floor and between.

Munching on my snack,
the finest pasty in the land,
enveloped in flavour,
that truly blew my mind,
for the first time in too long,
with clean air my lungs filled,
I found myself wishing,
this would never have to end.

So I laid down my pasty,
and took a moment to glow,
water beneath to the hills above,
my eyes wandered, my mind in tow,
time of reflection over,
I returned to my tasty snack,
only to find a seagull,
snapping it up behind my back.

Our eyes met, and we both knew,
there was a situation at hand,
if this were any other time, any other place,
said seagull would have met a timely end,
But not that day.

I looked at the scavenger,
with fire in my eyes,
but as I looked at him or her,
I was not inclined to check,
an understanding was reached,
at peace, at one with my surroundings,
I said, 'Go on Mr Seagull, you can have that one.'

Thomas Hutchinson

CELEBRATION

We choose to celebrate
when happening gives cause,
to party long and late.

It is our chosen fate
so thumbs down to the bores,
we choose to celebrate.

Whilst others may berate,
we will ignore the laws
to party long and late.

'Though we're in no fit state,
we'll open wide our doors,
we choose to celebrate.

When life's frustrations grate
our spirit soars
to party long and late.

No matter what the date
and almost without pause,
we choose to celebrate,
to party long and late.

Judith Blakemore Lawton

RECOVERY

I'm OK
I know you're sad
Pain will soon drift away
I'll be better
When I stop hiding the truth
I'll recover from the damage
I caused in my youth

No need to hide
It's time to talk
Don't fall foul to the urges
Like you've done before
It's time to play
It's your chance to start over today

You're so endearing
Without those drugs on your brain
Future highs
Are through natural means
No more dependencies
Or discrepancies
Over your failure to pay
Those bills on time

This is the start
It's about to begin
Stop living in the past
Of what could have been
You're now taking action
So let others in

Use your potential
Don't get sidelined
Focus on your present state of mind
No more wasted time
Those days are far behind

A promise to take this no further
So you won't hurt no more
And you'll hope to remember
That you don't need to inflict your drug
On the most important person of all

Wayne Glover

LIZZY DRIPPING

(Dedicated to my terminally ill sister. Her nickname is such because she is always working and cleaning, hence (dripping) sweating)

Lizzy Dripping, why do we call her this?
Well Elizabeth, Liz, whatever, she's our sis,
She was nicknamed this because it suits,
Not the ones you were with kinky boots.
No our Lizzy, she's elegant and smart
She's always had it right from the start.
If we call her Elizabeth you'll think of her royal,
Busy as a bee, cleaning all the time
Nothing's a toil
Her abode like herself is spic and span
From top to bottom, try to match her if you can.
Her wardrobe is full of nice attire
All her hangers are wood not wire,
But when worn by Lizzy Dripping
She's all class, you will have to travel far
To find such a lass
Her cooking is the same perfection,
Like her big heart is full of affection,
Lizzy Dripping can be deep in thought
Looking aloof, thinking about what she has bought,
Always organised, doing chores in advance,
Give her God and her good spirit another chance,
As she deserves it more than anyone I know,
Let her talents and abilities show,
She puts her family and friends at the top of her list,
So hear my prayers, I really insist,
I love my Lizzy Dripping like a lot of others do,
Long shall she remain to make an impact on me and you
She's strong and soft in equal parts,
She's our gorgeous sister and in our hearts.
Hers is a heart of gold, a precious metal that glows,
She melts ours, with the kindness she shows,
So now you know why we give her this name,
Elizabeth, Liz, Lizzy Dripping, she remains the same.

Alana Quinn

RECYCLED SKIN

A new mother slips two fingers through the blinds in the labour ward and parts them,
she looks at her newborn,
counts on her fingers all the things she hopes she has not passed down.
Her daughter has a birthmark of absence on her chest –
her mother doesn't know how to love something so like herself.

Nineteen years on –
her daughter stands at a front door of a house she has never lived in,
she is recycled skin and wants to trace the mangled trash that made her.
Histories are dirty muddied things.

Her mother parts her blinds in the same fashion – a woman of habit,
when she sees her child
she regrets not knowing how to swallow the space years create
into a conversation that means something.

There are limits to this language,
found in acrid mouths where apologies won't flower.

There are only so many times you can look at your mother
before you want to see the reverse of her sewn-up skin.
The girl's eyes target the caesarean scar she knows sits under the cardigan,
she wants to cut it clean again and crawl into the sin that made her.
In the last few years, her mother has become merely human,
with all the heaving weight that brings.

Our deepest parts are made from the things we'd rather forget.

She has been searching in her parents' parched mouths for parts of herself.

After having unpicked every fable her mother pressed into her questioning mouth,
she is asking for answers again.

What do you expect me to say?

List the reasons you forgot how to be a mother,
spittle gathers at the sides of her mouth,
this too will be feeble.
Your daughter is trying to be a lady,
but her legs learnt to stride like men
walking quickly away from difficult situations.

She has the face of a mother who left her,
wants men to wear her bruised skin inside their own
so she can be naked of every itch of heritage she cannot hunt down –
it does not work,
nobody loves someone who has loss etched on the underside of their tongue,
scared they will kiss away the ability to love from your lips.

You gamble days away with those lips
– use them for prayer, not to kiss broken things better.

She is holding her daughter's pummeling fists in the dim front room,
loneliness hangs in the very same place around their cheekbones,
she is you thirty years earlier –
brittle and hesitant to dream.

She will never know why leaving was easier than loving
but the past will draw vicious circles around the young if you let it.

It's difficult to allow yourself to understand those who hurt you,
and there are only so many ways of saying the same goddamn thing
but in the dip of the couch they are sharing,
they find a strength to crush years into recycled CD Roms,
archives of the past, and leave them glinting
by some wayside on a road your mother still refuses to name.

Aisling Fahey

THE ALLERGY CATS

I have a mother-in-law
She has free-roaming cats.
No room is out of bounds to her furry fiends.
Bedroom, kitchen, bathroom, study
Lounge paws clean, garden paws muddy.

Sleek and purring, rubbing, scratching
Clinging to corners,
Hiding from strangers.
Flurry of fur, saliva and dander
Spreading allergens here and yonder.

I am on the rebound
I recoil and react.
I splutter, cough, wheeze and sneeze.
I'm red-faced, can't breathe
My breast all a heave . . .

I have a mother-in-law
She has free-roaming cats.
So, for fear of symptoms taking hold
My visits are curtailed,
On account of the allergy cats.

Or am I allergic to my . . . ?

Julie Vouillemin

ONE DAY AS A LION

The mess that's grown limits, the escaping raw smell of old dishes,
door in, barred with junk mail and calling cards from pest control visits.
Domestic woe emits through a wall of amateur canvases as scraps of
tablature, matches and cobbled stanzas litter the floor with festival tickets.
Receptacles of viscous foreign matter sit near novelty finds,
as a toddler's keen smile shines from a photo to where Johnny reclines.
Half Pollock, the rest Sid Vicious, cap badge of a commie resides,
his doppelganger fracturing, Eskimo kissing that poverty line.
Body clock's time resets as shallow breathing heightens,
Irises dilate, cold sun rising in his sinus.
Nervous system becomes aroused, takes account, grows reliant,
as the heart's given the same regard as any other household appliance.
Reel-to-reel breaks the silence with the beat loop of a track,
as Johnny jams bass lines started three moons back.
Feeling at teeth loose, he tweaks the levels and EQ,
knowing the routine, if he's to sleep soon it'll be through tranqs.

See the speed's crude wrap, thinks, *you've got habit's greed to thank*
for the bandaged deep wound, tank that leaks fuel and leaves you strapped.
Cupboards empty, pockets brasic, the repeat use trap,
promising self freedom, after a stop off at the garage and Pete's new flat.
Passing the petrol pumps he holds his spot, cotching, placid,
keeping cool, watching traffic. The queue builds and blocks the passage
of sight to the back, so with sleight of hand, food's copped with magic
and he's off the forecourt before anyone clocks what just happened.
Then at the next shop along the block, microwaves what he's robbed
and jogs round to knock at Pete's, check if he's in or not.
That's where I knew him from. Friend of a friend lived next door
and we'd listen to his codswallop monologues while he waited in the warm.
The path Johnny walked society saw as asinine,
far cry from the paradigm of a nine-to-five corporate ladder rise,
but he bore the kind of compacted spine you'd find touring the poorest factory lines,
brought with exhaustive practice time, absorbed till morning's crack of light.

Falling worn, an expanded mind, courting madness while the raptures climbed,
forfeiting that standard ride, to pour all into his grand designs,
he sacrificed: two point four kids, a mortgage,
trophy wife to get divorced with and Boss to lash the horsewhip,
just to have his time and the little support he was awarded.
Knowing the sad demise, how cancer thrives when distracted by that captive's life.
That plasticized plant pot on the desk is an active sign
of why office workers in cubicles stare at horizons all cadaver-eyed.
It's the line between safety and risk, whether you existed or lived,
why the senile are haunted by the dreams they had as kids.
It's Icarus, flying and falling, taking jumps from great heights,

it's one day as a lion; Johnny's heart exploding as he slept that night.
Reception site for the funeral was a forest building where, bathed in light,
we were met inside by his music filling the acoustics as mates arrived.
So lucid in the aisles, belated truth became decaying smiles,
surrounding by his paintings and the pages he scribed compiled.

Friends and family filed in and met local bands and kids,
as the speaker took the stand to mark the death of an anarchist.
'The many lives,' he said, 'The talented, multifaceted,
diversity of those in attendance, testament to the fact of it.'
Saying, 'How sad is it, to think we're accurate when we act critic on road.
When of even those closest, we know just a fraction of the soul.'
He said, 'You'll find a map to Johnny in the protagonists he wrote,
between the drum rolls and hushed notes in the tracks that he composed,
in the gusto of the brush strokes, within canvases on show
and through your anecdotes disclosed, so will that labyrinth become known.'
The trap I'd inhabited as home, fell with a question I couldn't pass, less
I answered what I'd do with my life if I had ten years till last breath.
Now with two rotations around our closest star left, I dedicate this
not just to Johnny the artist, but to how life departed with him,
because for eight years, I've poured my heart into every page of bars I've written
and it's only now I'm learning to hold a piece back to impart to the art of living.

Joe Coghlan

SWEET TEMPTATION

Harvesting something sweet and delicious,
My hand grapples through the small opening.
This is what it is like to be truly hungry,
To have the scent wash your nostrils dry.

I push further inside, my heart quickening,
The low level humming warns of the guards at their posts.

Delighted – I have reached it.
I poke my hand further, lick my lips and retrieve my prize.
Yet, the gold weighs heavy in my palm, for I have robbed a bank.

Sophia Clemans (18)

ANOTHER DRINK

Windswept, tears fall
Silent steps in a dim lit hall.
All alone, full of regret
Too many things she can't forget.
Harsh words, so quickly said
Blurry eyes and a hazy head.
Another drink, she fills her glass
Wishing time, would quickly pass.

Thinking through, the evening's events
Knowing that she never meant
To destroy, what they had built
Wrapped up in her duvet of guilt.
Still cold, she lies down,
In the bed in her dressing gown.
Wide awake, she can't sleep
Her heart so heavy, she begins to weep.

Heavy breathing, a restless night
Dreams plagued with the vicious fight.
Red Hand, she slapped his face
Feeling her heart begin to race
Adrenaline surge. It got heated,
Yet her heart was torn, her emotions depleted.
Cold eyes, this was the end
His broken heart she could not mend.

She chose to throw it all away
For another man, come what may
Drunk, sex, a stupid mistake
That's all it took, to easily break
Their love, their wedding vows
Despite their regular arguments and rows.
This hurt. He can't forgive her.
He may still love her but there's too much anger.

Gemma Perrott

THROUGH MY EYES

Fire, blood, carnage and war
Raiding our fertile historical land
We ran with fear in our eyes
Just like the African lion,
On the hot, dry Savannah
It chases the defenceless zebra
Just like they did to us, attacking the innocent

Fire, blood, carnage and war
Burning our homes and other gnomes
We fled with anxiety in our veins
Just like the hermit crustacean
Crawling on the ocean floor
It leaves its home for another shell
Just as we had to leave, we left our memories

Fire, blood, carnage and war
Fighting our people, even our steeple
We tried to fight with our hearts
They were like a pack of wolves
Hunting in violent numbers
They treated us like pieces of meat
Just like pieces of nothing, they had no remorse

Through my eyes
They looked anarchic and cold
Aggressive and lawless
There seemed no written law.
They were the Vikings without fear.

Martin Schwartz

PLATE-CARRYING SKUM

I am a member of the minimum wage brigade,
Working in a non-skilled trade.
I am carrying your plate, pouring the wine for your dinner date
Whilst inside I am planning my escape.

I smile apologetically as you complain that your food is late,
But behind my mask I am reaming with hate for your upper class snobby traits.

I am just plate-carrying skum,
Society labels me as dumb.
But at least I'm not just sitting on my bum.

Underpaid, underappreciated and struggling to find the rent,
When payday comes every penny is already spent.

It has gone two in the morning as I scribble my rants onto paper;
Another night of no sleep as my brain works overtime,
Consequence of a chaotic mind.

Years of smoking way too much dope,
Has led to a frustration of wasted youth and lost hope.

Tomorrow morning back to the daily chores,
A long list of repetitive bores,
Scrubbing dirty floors and cleaning down greasy doors.
Pretending I give a shit, I just wanna roll on the floor and throw a fit.

Cos everything is so repetitive, and I get bored,
Bored to tears.
Only been doing this job four months,
But it feels like a million years.

I need to use my brain,
Otherwise I'm gunna go insane.
Like this I am wasted,
My creativity has no outlet.
Causing a madness inside,
Almost considering sticking pins in my eyes.

Because, I am a member of the minimum wage brigade,
Working in a non-skilled trade.

Hayley Hudson

KIND CLOUDS

Only half in common
We're only part entwined;
Broken-hearted history
I'm left to romanticise.

We exist independently,
But you're there when I look behind
At our unfinished addition
To the passages of time.

I don't recall making snowmen,
Or splashing puddles in the rain;
It's the absence of your memory
That keeps me perplexed in pain.

But as I weep in the downpour,
I bitter-sweetly realise
A humble, evanescent comfort
Which can dry tears from my eyes:

The rain which merges with my tears
Will endure evaporation
And soothe you as you cry yourself:
The process repeats via precipitation.

Thus, we may not have the past,
But the clouds which sit above
While taking pity on my plight;
Allow us to share some love.

But faith in clouds is hard to keep;
For now I'm filled with doubt.
No rain is falling to connect us,
So I'm trapped in perpetual drought.

R. Haughton

WHAT IF . . .

the grass will never get
any greener than this
and there will be no sweeter sound
than the water's dragging hiss
as it slopes back over pebbles
rolled between its fingertips?

What if it will get no more
beautiful, no, or dramatic
than the showy crest of a wave
running home from the Atlantic
as it folds and beaks its back
against the beach, well, what if

I have seen all the colours of the sky
no sun that sets will do it any brighter
no colour spilled on the horizon
will be new or unfamiliar,
and the bluest of summer days
will never get any bluer?

Will it never get any sweeter at all
than the arching bough of a tree
or the skylark's playful call
as it lifts and lifts on the
morning's warm thermals,
well, what if it will get

No more pleasing to the eye
than the twisting aerobatics
of a gaggle of starlings passing by
or of a solitary hawk up there
slowly climbing high
until it is all but lost to gravity?

Well, what if there will be
no more glorious sight
than a single ruffled cloud
in a high windblown flight
or the blinking of the stars
on a cold clear night?

What if my life has been
at its most romantic
and I have had my share of love
neither frenzied nor tantric
and all those beauties have
passed me by, well, what if

There will be no sweeter sound
than the water's dragging hiss
as it slopes back over pebbles
rolled between its fingertips
and the grass will never get
any greener than this?

Jonathan Inder

ALL EYES ON US

The London 2012 Olympics are here at last,
The opening ceremony gripped the nation's heart,
Team GB's medal haul was slow at first,
But you could feel the athletes' determination and thirst.

And soon the gold medals started flooding in,
As British athletes secured a win,
From cycling to rowing and judo too,
Boxing, equestrian and athletics went through.

The Olympic Park was a feast for the eyes,
The volunteers were cheery and on a high,
The stadium lit up and the crowd went wild,
As the Olympic Games were embraced by man and child.

With home advantage, we wanted to do our best,
And our city and transport were certainly put to the test,
But we shone and we did ourselves proud,
Leaving a lasting impression on the global crowd.

So keep the Union Jack flying high,
It's Great Britain's chance to shine,
The whole world is watching us in awe,
Take a bow London, this is our floor.

Melanie Dayasena-Lowe

PHOTOGRAPH: A POEM IN TWO STYLES, OF TWO MOMENTS, SEPERATED BY TWO DECADES

i) The giving of it

Don's cup evokes a clown's nose full of tea.
Loose talk lines crack like eggs on dragging skin.
My uncle reaches; red eyes zooming in
I watch his wrist of Chinese stainless steel,
then take the photo time once took of me
who winced to see one still so young and thin
as printed paper, that I can't begin
to touch again the harbour wall or sea:

where waves and gulls, immune from sweet decay
lie frozen flat to August – twenty years –
pickled in gloss to wait on Weston Bay,
tAke bAck iTunes, iPads, eBay, iSay,
till towers, planes and Britpop pass my ears,
and let me salmon swim back – to that day.

ii) The examination of it

Deep steep shadows are things I notice last:
a gauze before the stone sea wall to cool the insect cracks,
echoing Jet's dark canine shape
on the ice cream flavoured floor.
A long tongue dripping drool.
Should Jet shake his jowls, we'll dip and duck,
but he's a statue –
with streaming sun etched upon his ebony fur and paws.

John, my father, holds the Great Dane's hungry head.
Our backs face Steep Holm Island, where starved Vikings fell – unfed.
Everything's packed in a fat blue
bag with sugar-coated coats,
resting on shoes of suede.
Should John move, sweets will scatter and fly
but he's a clock stayed –
with creases set in concrete on his T-shirt and rock jeans.

Me? I'm smiling – like an anchor – fussing Jet.
I'll wreck these black sunglasses in the ocean – though not yet.
First we'll follow fast fried fishes
past the causeway's tide-worn chips,
skimming the sea dog's shells.
But I gaze at me through two decades:
that buoy who never changed
and yet I'm here: the paradox in photographs is clear.

B A Huckfield

RAVEN

Oh Bird, take flight on wing,
As black as your voice that calls to me,
And take my letter to a land unseen,
Far where the shrieking wind will sing,
And night is all that we may see.

For your feathers are but of deep ebony,
Your eyes alight with intelligence beneath,
A mask you wear filled with a curious stare,
To deceive and know who will be next,
To transverse the distances which leave people vexed.

For now to travel to the land of despair,
Where souls will call for the peace of sleep,
But alas I must now but know,
Before my buds of sorrow flourish and grow,
If she made the journey there all safe,
And rests remembering of a life well lived and faced.

So go dark creature, go!
With your fiery eyes and wings unfold,
Go where no mortal must ever tread,
For there will be no rest for me in the land of the living,
If she cannot rest in the land of the dead.

Zoe Davis

PROPER GAMMY PIGEON

I saw a weak bird hopping
on one claw because the other
had become a red ball at the end
of its leg, I couldn't
help, but think of blisters and
sprained ankles and hunger pain
as it pecked at a discarded potato
skin on the floor, I wanted to
kiss it, to suck the pus and
poison from its body and
spit it into the face of fate.

I don't know what to call this feeling.

I heard a drunk man in a beer garden talking
about how he cut his body with clippers,
trying to remove his body of black
curly hairs. He advised razors instead and
I looked at his baby in its pram and I thought of my
friend pressing hot curlers onto her arm when he spoke about
the blood dripping down his trouser leg.
I stopped smoking my cigarette and
thought about my body.

I don't know what to call this feeling.

All at once dead foxes,
Sunsets,
the relentless ivy on bricks,
broken collar bones,
stepping on plugs,
magnolia leaves,
roast lamb.

I do not feel infinite.

Hannah Locke

ANGST

No one looks beyond
The wild, fearful eyes
No one takes the time needed
To wait for hesitant –
Output.
So they judge me,
Turn quickly away
To spare their precious time
leaving me
Defeated.
All except
Those wily, cunning ones
Who quietly coax my knowledge
And use it as their own
Why not? – who else would believe
That this pathetic, stammering wretch
Had anything credible or worthy
To suggest?

Later – alone
I cherish the thought
That my concept
Had been used and acted upon
Even though I have no claim to fame
I know and glow inside
And my angst dissolves,
If only for a short while
And my life looks out
Through a window of gold.

Josephine Sawley

WALKING ON COLLAPSING BONES

I had this weird dream – or a vision I should say,
That I had on these grey skyscraper ankle boots,
walking on the moon with footprints,
relaying the message that 'with Christ, the sky is never the limit'.

And I had a soul with a life line long enough to praise Him,
And I carried a vessel big enough for God to reside in.
And God was close enough that my soul could taste Him,
because He was closer than my breath is.

The moon, the stars, the sun, let alone the wind, didn't age,
And death couldn't kill true beauty like our souls,
or a memory or His word that never fails.

Or the simple word from my mum,
'Tayo no forget for pray-oh!
Don't forget to pray.'

It was beauty personified in everything:
The yous and mes,
The praise in our pain,
The tears in our joy,
Nothing was taken for granted.

In this place

Even though we sin,
We walk on collapsing bones seeking repentance,
And not blame the Eve for taking a bite,
but thanking our Christ for sacrificing more than His hands just so He can hug us.

We praised the moments for the Tree that was cut down to a Cross,
and the Cross that stood there as a signpost to love and freedom.

A love,
A love that was hard and tender,
'Cause our loving got bones too delicate to gloat on
and it would be too easy to choke on

Why did I ever forsake Him?
And limit myself to a flesh so weak that,
it disembodied the Holy Spirit in me?

Chasing kisses and infidelity,
tying my flesh to another woman's misery.
Staining their beautiful memories,
Adding affliction to them by lying with them and leaving after the fix,
all because I have forsake You,
And follow flesh wretched enough to curse me.
Foolishly I knew the world so I birthed its curse.

I still do walk these dark paths,
The only difference is, God has been the shining rock
that breaks the darkness for which I have to repent constantly.

Constantly be on my knees,
So often the Earth embraced my kneecaps.

He would lift me up to a song,
And I'd be dancing in His amazing grace,
like I've got some of Solomon's electric melodies within my bones.

Things do fall apart but we walk hand in hand with the Creator,
And wherever I stand will praise Him.
Even though my flesh may lie,
I will speak through my soul
And with every human, I will read the sign they walk with:
Caution, handle with care.
For He is in us,
and we are too fragile to stand alone but too strong to break us.

Let's praise Him in our moments,
Praise Him in our hymns,
Let's praise.

Julian Knox

EMBRACING THE STOP

When life isn't working
You can try and slow down
But I find it's hard to slow down
When I've already stopped
And then when I know that I've already stopped
It's then when I want to press start.

So Instead of hitting the start
One day I opted for pause
Stopping the tape
And making the break
From warring jibber jabber
Banging round in my head

Then dropping into silence, and
Embracing the stop
I found the clear still voice
The space within.

Alexander Buchan

STOLEN SOHILA

First you say yes, then you say no, then you say stop, then you say go
Then your inner strength is going, going, gone,
And you're out the door
And nothing means anything anymore
You want to carry on
Think you can grow, I can see you have lost your get up and go
I call and call and call
It's like a deserted long hall
I worry you may have had a fall
The voice in my head
Says *are you alive or dead?*
I lie thinking in my bed
Everything that you have ever said
Your body frail and thin
I bet you're drinking gin
This is such a sin
Passers-by stop, look at you and stare
But I know you don't really care
You're not happy, you're just existing
We are being torn apart
Like the board from its thrown dart
You are living your life in a mist
And have taken enough abuse from the fist
This is not living
The Devil has you by the hand
And you think he is your friend
And you give him a grand
Take the crack and heroin from his hand
Bury your head in the sand
He's celebrating his life in his hands
Gold paved streets are at his feet
He is greeting everyone so sweet
And you are just a slave to his every beat
Living a life full of defeat
You cannot eat, you cannot sleep
I'm weeping, crying
Whilst you're high, sighing
I feel you're slowly dying
You're continually lying
I'm still crying, you never pick up the phone
Like a dog without a bone
Whilst you carry on buying more and more
Until you're on the floor
And everything you love is out the door

I'm feeling a bore
I can hardly watch this anymore
Whilst people are taking advantage of you
You're still inhaling more
Throwing up and being sick
You're the one taking all the licks
I feel sicker than sick
You're still going strong
Your night is young
Your party is your own song
And this is where you feel like you belong
And sing to Michael Jackson
Beat It, like you own the song
I know you long for more
I just want to open up the door of happiness
Instead of sadness
This lifestyle is madness
Tears full of laughter
Please God, make it happy ever after
You are more than a grafter, you are smarter
I would award you a BAFTA
I feel like I'm in the movie of disaster
And life is getting faster,
Now I give you the degree of honours, Masters
Stop this, 20 years have passed us
Has a spell been cast
Or a curse burdened from your purse?
It's ridiculous, this is longer than any religious fast
This is not just a starter
I don't know how your stomach takes the main and after
This isn't a life full of laughter
It's outrageous and full-blown contagious
You can still be a genius
Study the galaxies
And astrophotography
Take your mind to explore
Delve into much higher than before
Believe me you don't need drugs anymore
You're bright, clever and adored
Please don't be bored
I treasure you more than the Queen's jewels
Our love is more than any alcoholic measure
I'm sure we can turn this round into pleasure

You are my lost and found treasure,
Together forever, you are my long-lost star sister, Stolen Sohila.

Mouna Goldy

THE STOLEN CAR

It came as quite a shock to me
To see how much can fit into
A stolen car;
First four adolescent boys
With their assorted teenagers' toys:
GameBoy, boombox, serrated blade,
A baby cocktail made of something
Sweet to rot the teeth, mixed in with
Cider, rotgut cheap, or cut price vodka
If mum's stumped up that week,
Now add to this four egos
So swollen with testosterone
That one alone would
Fill the Albert Hall;
Then squeeze in several pounds
Of Macho pride,
A smear of anger, angst
And along just for the ride
An ounce or two or fear.
Then if it's a sunny day
Along the way they may
Pick up a pair of babes,
Thus over-lifted tits and processed hair
Must be shoehorned in somewhere;
Youth takes up a lot of space.

The car is now abandoned
On the corner of my road,
Really I should say remains
It ain't a car no more:
No windows, doors, the seats ripped out,
Its dereliction is complete
As it squats gutted on my street
Stinking of burnt joys.
I guess that no one died this time,
Despite the concertinaring
And the bloodstains on the dash,
If it had been a fatal crash
It would have worn a shroud of tarp
Before being towed away
By police who then would
Play at science.

Now its only passengers are
Three bursting bin bags, one smashed TV
A broken chair and,
Most strange of all to me,
The limb ripped from a young oak tree;
We've been planting trees in Hackney
To make the ghetto green.

Youth takes up a lot of space.

Annie Byfield

HAVE YOU EVER?

Have you ever told the truth
But no one believes?
Because of no evidence to bring to light, you see.

Have you ever felt so low
Time went by, you didn't know?
A lot of your friends and family really phonies vanished.

Have you ever laughed so much?
People say you're happy all the time.
But never realise the pain, hurt and confusion that grows within you.
Burning like fire inside.

Have you ever been so ignored, so hurt and so abused to the full
That you're tired of calling for help?
You cried so much.
Now you're so emotionally numb, so distant, all your tears subside.
You can't feel anything.
Resentment, it's not worth it.
And now you wish you would just die.

Have you ever stopped and stared into the distance?
Suicide thoughts.
Nothing nice to share.

Have you ever?
When before you felt so high.

Louise Martika Michel Roseman

ALONE, BUT NOT FOR LONG

As you slept on
I cried
Alone in my thoughts, in a sea of people
Life rushes by, I felt lost for a moment
Sad and alone

But alone, I liked it
Grounded in the moment
Perspectives lay bare

No matter who,
Or what,
There will always be a problem
It's nature,
Who we are,
What we live for

Alone in my thoughts, and I liked it

Lorraine Wood

LOVE

Love is found in most towns
In young and old alike
When he is away time drags
When he is near it is a lovely feeling
Looks in eyes give warmth to cold and stubborn hearts.

You try desperately to please each other
One often succeeds, the other dismally fails
The way he walks and what he wears
Who are his friends and where he lives
You name these all
You know in your heart that he is yours forever.

Susan Maxwell

CHILDHOOD MEMORIES

I loved the smell of summer
Hot pavements, melting tar
Tea is almost ready
We play, but never far

We play in streets free of cars
Hopscotch, tag and such
We only dash for safety
As here comes Bevan's bus

A bumblebee is buzzing
And butterflies alight
Oh so many colours
I'm dazzled by the sight

I loved the smell of autumn
Of Mornings cool and clear
Old apples hanging from the trees
New term, new school, new fear

That special smell of leather
Black polished shoes and belt
A satchel Nan has bought me
Brand new, how proud I felt

Then winter bursts upon the scene
The smells have changed again
Bonfires and frosty walkways
Roasting chestnuts in the rain

The spicy smells of Christmas
Puddings, cakes and such
Pink sugar mice, pine trees
And parcels we mustn't touch

Then spring steps gently into sight
All senses are alert
New summer shoes are purchased
White socks and coloured skirts

The rain is warm not heavy
The smells are fresh and clean
And everyone is happy
In my far off childhood dream.

Barbara Brimble

THE DARKNESS IN TIME

There's a moment of darkness that lies in a black hole
It gets in your head and it won't let go
At your lowest point thoughts appear that just aren't you
But at that time it makes perfect sense to follow through

It's like you're in so deep however hard you climb
You can't see that light
It's just pitch-black and cloudy grey on the inside
I've been there, I've felt that loneliness,
That harrowing pain
The kind that strips away who you are
So you're never the same
Sometimes I've wished I wasn't here
Just so it'd be easier to live without that fear

It's scary to lose parts of myself I thought I once knew
Who am I? Why am I here? Why do I do what I do?
I breakdown, get lost, feel myself losing grip
I can no longer be in this reality I'm in

I always believed I'd never make it through
On some level I wasn't really good enough too
The hurt just flows out of my heart like a river
And worst part is most of the time I'm the trigger

I make myself feel these things that consume my soul
I'm trapped walking down a path to the wrong way home
Help me please, I'm down on my knees, I want out
I'm stood in a deserted field, I scream, I shout

Someone might as well have ripped out every organ I have
My body lives lifeless, too motionless to stand
What if I can't ever get back who I was,
What I wanted to be?
What if I'm stuck with this girl who is no longer me.

Katie Reed

JUST LOOK AROUND

Just look around, tell me what do you see?
I see a world full of opportunity, a place to make my stand and live out my dreams, as best I planned,
But truth is we are sinking quicker than quicksand, but beforehand, everyone was proud of their homeland.
Now everyone's either angry or sad and to be honest it's like the whole world has gone mad.
We got leaders trying to dictate instead of innovate and educate, misusing their powers, but when it comes to the crunch they're all a bunch of cowards.
I see everyone as equal, so tell me, who in their right mind would kill their own people!
Now we got youths thinking it's cool to carry a tool to school, or may it's for protection, but either way, we need to establish a connection for a positive direction, shoot for the stars and aim for perfection.
At the moment we've got young sons with knives and guns, babies having babies, under-aged mums. Mixed in the pot with the rise of inflation, now everyone's feeling stressed out in this situation.
The temperature's getting hot, you can feel the heat.
I hear people say,
'What's the point?' It's like everyone's embracing defeat.
I often hear the silent cry, as I sit and watch the world go by.
Can't get a job, not even if they try. So they look to rob or shoot drugs to get by.
but a focused mind is unstoppable and if we can't do it, then it must be impossible.
A chance begins with us, so we gotta see things clearer and like MJ said, it starts with the man in the mirror.

Soul Urban Poet

HARVEST OF MEN

In the harvest of men, men fall and rise like winter wheat
Some will be forgotten, some remembered
Some will never exist, some will die before existence
Some will die victorious, some will die trying
Some conquer, while some are conquered
Some fall apart, while some rise still
Some believe fate chooses destiny by the character of men, while some have none
Some believe if you make patience a quality and beauty a mentality then you make life a reality.

Hamza Rasul

CALLUM'S WORDS TO MUMMY

(Dedicated to Leah Johnson, who tragically lost her little boy, Callum, to SIDS (Sudden Infant Death Syndrome) on 16/3/12 aged 17 months and 1 week)

As he walks through the gates of Heaven,
God smiles and holds him tight.
'Don't worry my child,' He whispers,
'Walk into my light.'
He takes a step and glances back,
With a hint of a tender tear.
'Don't fear my child,' God says to him,
'For one day your loved ones will be here.'

'There's lots of pretty flowers,
There's lots of toys here too,
I'm playing in Heaven's garden
And there's lots of angels too!'

'Please don't worry Mummy
I truly am OK,
God told me I'm only here on loan,
And you'll join me here one day.
Until that day arrives,
You have to carry on,
Just smile each day and think of me,
I'll be in your heart where I belong.'

Janine Osborne

SEVEN LIVES

You have survived seven crashes on seven motorbikes,
Ascended seven times to the ceiling
And pitied seven dying bodies beneath you.
You have astonished seven consultants (who dislike being astonished),
Spoken with seven angels who tried to coax you home,
Preserved seven grafts of skin like relics
And, this morning, blessed seven roses with holy water
And forced out seven words I understand:
Motorbike, bungalow, mother, garden, flowers, trees, Philip.

Peter Adair

THE SOLDIER

The soldier stands alone staring at the sun
He watches it rising into the sky, another day begun.
He walks alone, his shadow cast behind him
With an emptiness within.
In his uniform head held high
A solitary bird on the wing passes by
In his heart he has a love waiting at home
He can't wait to hear her voice when he picks on the phone.
When he sees her he will hold her forever close, forever tight,
Loving her gently all through the night
He dreams of those day in the desert heat
While he kicks up the sand with his weary feet
He can almost hear her voice gently whisper in his ear
As if she is next to him leaning near
Saying, 'I may not be there in body but always in spirit and just to let you know
I am with you wherever you go.'

Ann Rowlinson

TAP-RAP

Show them what you're made of,
Do that thing you do,
Keep it sharp and shiny
Never dull, and blue.

People stop to listen,
When you start to sing,
People start tap-rapping,
When you do that thing.

No one does it better
You can show the way,
Till they're all tap-rapping,
Tap-rapping every day.

Jean Robertshaw

13TH OF NOVEMBER 2008

13th of November 2008
Is not for me just a date.
My eyes wide open what a sight
To finally see what life is like.

I was so naïve to think he'd stay,
As in the end we're all taken away.
I thought like a toy he'd be fixed
For this childhood game is now in bits.

I'd look for an excuse not to go, in vain
For I couldn't bring myself to see his pain.
But now I finally want to go, I'd kill
For the chance but never will.

When you come of age they welcome you to adulthood
But is there a sell by date on your childhood?
Its events we are unable to control
That will determine our growth to unfold.

13th of November 2008
Is not for me just a date
The pain, the anger, I'm misunderstood
For now I am a part of this adulthood.

Samantha Lewtas

OUR JUST DESERTS

Is all of life but random risk?
A chance indiscriminate gamble?
Rodent-controlled on computed disc
In a sliding cursor scramble?

Or logically led by rational genes?
Whose programmed genetic decree,
Equates by altruistic means,
All life's collective destiny?

Is our circus rehearsed already?
Re-fated or Russian roulette?
Do the lucky ones win the teddy
Or do we deserve what we get?

Doris Hallpike

BE HAPPY WITH THE SIMPLE THINGS IN LIFE

Will we ever be happy with what we have till it's gone?
The walks in the park
The ducks and the geese
The fish in the ponds
Picnics and feasts

The ice cream van that plays out a song
The sun on our backs as we're walking along
School holidays, midsummer breaks
Days by the seaside, boats on the lake

Fairgrounds and rides
Games, win a prize!
Hot dogs and onions
Burgers, French fries

The cows and the sheep
The horse in the field
Everyday farm life
Windmills' big wheels

Clouds just like cotton
Birds in the air
Scarecrows with hats on
Hay for their hair

The good things in life
The people we know
Places we've been to and places we go.
So don't take for granted the everyday things
Count each day as a blessing the good that life brings.

John Morris

GUARDIAN ANGEL

An angel came into my dream today
But as it came closer it slowly faded away

An angel with no wings, it was ailed
It was a guardian angel who had failed

She came up to me and asked me
If I could watch over she

For years she was left alone
No one could hear her moan

For he had failed to protect her
From the corruption of this world as it were

And so he came to me
He knew that I could see

At first I thought he was wrong
But he told me I was strong

And so I didn't flee
But swore to protect her with the light inside me . . .

Tracy Humphreys

LOVE

The touch of his hand on mine
The smile on his face when we embrace
The passion I feel whenever he's near
I feel like a schoolgirl with her first crush
I want to make him happy, maybe I try too hard
I try to control my feelings but I just can't comprehend
The way he sends such love to me
That's the way I feel about him
They say it's wrong because I'm a man
But yes it's love
Crazy love
Passionate love
Maybe it's hopeless love
But it's all the love I need.

H A Finnah

WALKIES

Trotting gaily by the window go the doggies on their leads,
Off upon their daily jaunt to crap beneath the trees,
Or on pavements, footpaths, roads;
It doesn't really matter where the doggies dump their loads.
Heads held and tails aquiver
As they shit down by the river.
Haunches taut and eyes glazed over
They squat: meantime the owner,
Looks away and scuffs the dirt,
Pretends the doggy isn't theirs,
Whistles, and when all is done,
Throws a stick,
The doggy's gone!
Leaving behind for our delight
Another, steaming pile of shite.
Dawn and dusk oh please beware
That is when the owners dare
To step into the murky mists
And leave their little doggy gifts:
Gifts that blind the tiny children
Who in innocence step in 'em.
When I'm king and have a whip
Each owner'll get a cocktail stick
And have to scrape each nook and cranny
End eat it all in a dog turd sarnie,
Gagging as it hits the throat
And vomit smears their walking coat.
Enough! You know I'll not shut up,
For fuck's sake, clean your dog's shit up!

Jean Westwater

SARA

You are a defenceless small island, yet so majestic,
Your summits go impetuously through clouds' seas;
In a lands handful there is compressed
An enormous diversity of ecosystems.
In a day you can have sunny summer in a place,
Dark cold winter with snow thrashing heights,
Rain and clouds intensifying . . .

I am fortunate for your precious light's quality:
Clean skies of incredibly blue shades,
Forests filtering light,
Gullies drenched in your light.

Your light seeps in through clouds;
It bathes beaches, mountains;
It uncovers textures of sand dunes,
Colouring the dusk and dawn of rocks.

You are a paradise for the light lover,
Your poems just a shade of your quantity of variations,
Of an intimate encounter with the light.

Miriam Mesa

STEVEN ANDERSON

It is a warm summer's day,
Steven is a young lad of 24 years of age.
He is on his way to London
By National Express coach.

Steven arrives at around midday.
Over the road from the coach station,
There is the Café Rouge,
Upstairs from the shopping mall.

As Steven ascends the escalator
He is overwhelmed by the French ambience,
The accordion music, the waitresses,
The bistro wall lights
And the smell of fresh bread.

Scott Hanyours

THE PERPETUAL CONVERSATION

'Where's my wallet and keys?
Where you left them!'
'No they're not, you've moved them!'
'OK then, so where did you leave them?'
'Oh, I don't know now cos you've moved them!'
'Your problem is you've got no system,
That's why you always miss them.
If you hung your keys on a hook,
You wouldn't have to look.
Use that one by the front door,
Then put your wallet in your bedside drawer.
Your life would have a lot less frustration,
And we wouldn't keep having this conversation!
And you're too quick to go off crook,
Before you've had a proper look.
Where are my glasses? You once said,
And all the time they were on your head.
Then there's that other continual moan,
I can't find my mobile phone!'
Does all this sound familiar?
We've all heard it or something similar.
In households throughout the nation,
It is the perpetual conversation.
The quest for lost keys, wallet, glasses or mobile phone.
I have it almost daily in my own,
Which really is a worry, cos I live alone!

Dave Thomson

PRESENT FROM A FRIEND

What will you hold for me,
Beautiful bowl that you are?
Parcelled in the dark
You've come a long way.
Did you hear vans starting up?
Drivers shouting?
Did you travel by train,
Whirra, whirra, rumble, rumble –
Or hear the engines power up
And feel the plane accelerate?
Snug in your bubble wrap,
Inside your shoebox,
Did you feel the surge of take-off?
Were you shaken in bumpy air?
At the end of it all
You came to me,
I unwrapped you in a different daylight,
A new place,
Welcome beautiful bowl.

Lorna Ross

FOR CRYING OUT LOUD!

Oh! The pain in my neck
Makes me shout by heck,
Here I am with a stick.
That's my knee, did you hear it click?
I'll do my daily twists and turns, if I may
See if it takes my pain away.
The doctor said, 'You should stay in bed
Or take these tablets three times a day.'
I said, 'Dear Doctor, don't be cross,
I'm afraid I will have those tablets to toss,
My pain, it is not going away
I am nearly 82 years, it's here to stay.'

Maybe I am too old to be on the stage
So I will wave goodbye and end this rival rage.

Barbara Frances Ward

SKY OF CRIMSON

I like to meander to
Roam if you will, the countryside.

To mingle with the pure fresh air
And step on that grass so green.

And witness those giant yet humble trees
Arranged so beautifully, so wise.

Those buttercups and butterflies,
Oh and yes bees, somehow
Complementing each other with their roles
Roles they played to perfection.

This was a midsummer's evening
And all was tranquil.

Suddenly I glanced upwards
And there I saw it.

A breathtaking sky of crimson
Captured my eye and my senses.

It was a sky which held many a fair dream.
Dreams which it would not share
Somehow shy of expressing.

But then I didn't really mind,
As long as I had the chance to explore
And fulfill my feelings.

Above all, with a restful soul
A soul at peace for now.

Garry Mitchell

PEACE BY THE RIVER

Whispering grass, the wind in the willows
The river flows gentle streams, trickling of water,
Blue skies, jet streams, magpies, blackbirds, a thrush,
Life is slow here, a small boat floats by empty.

Is that an otter I see? The sun shines brightly,
Rabbits jumping or are they hares?
Crickets cricketing, frogs croaking, colourful dragonflies,
A flock of geese disturbs the peace, beautiful noise.

I'll have a sandwich and a cup of tea, maybe a biscuit or three
We will see peace at last
Open the newspaper, it's only good enough for chips
The freckles on my arms, damn, a fly in my eye.

Mud on my boots, let's go for a walk
Imprints the shape of my soles spreading outwards
I should have brought my rod, catch some fish
All the trees stand silently as if in the military.

That crossword is hard in my puzzle book
I've been here for hours now time to move on
Off home I go, what a lovely day by the river
Whose boat was that? I thought eating my dinner.

Kevin Dunbar

TOMORROW

The unspoken truth, a soul too precious for this world,
Silently, cruelly taken before our love fully unfurled,
The clock ticked menacingly as borrowed time faded,
Now I'm misplaced and alone; frozen in yesterday.

Today an all-consuming fire destroys my heart's charred remains,
Suffering imminent sorrow laced with searing pain,
A fleeting goodbye before we were deceitfully parted,
As my fragile heart shattered and perpetual tragedy started.

Though I remain cloaked in darkness,
Over fear, I retain one small advantage,
The certainty that death will face its demise,
And tomorrow we'll be back hand in hand, watching the last sunrise.

Pamela Davies

STEFFI!

A little girl she came to me
She came from the sky above
This little girl, this lovely girl
She filled my heart with love.

It was at a time in my life
My heart was not abundant
I'd been in a job for 25 years
And now I'd been made redundant.

To top it all, the very same week
There came another setback
There I was in a hospital ward
With a major heart attack.

It was then this girl, she came to me
It surely was truly fate
She came to me when I needed her
And I knew it was not too late.

We've been together now for many a year
We're truly so in love
This little girl, this lovely girl
Who came from the sky above.

Dave Williams

PERSEVERANCE

P atience can be hard, especially when you're on the ropes
E nergy is hard to muster when you're bereft of hope
R emember though, that every tunnel and journey has an end
S tand your ground, and good fortune will one day be your friend
E ndurance can be tough, I know that better than anyone
V ery well then, have a cry, but now there's work to be done!
E ach day brings you closer to the goal you're aiming for
R emember that you need a key to open every door
A lways keep going forwards, keep moving on
N ever give despair a chance to think that it has won
C almly and deliberately, you must persevere
E ventually you will succeed, and all the clouds will clear.

Christine Low

THEN . . . LIFE!

The sun is warm
The weather forecast true
At the back
A green patch
To sit and reflect
Age is 40
Life has begun
Fearing it before
Those eyes opened
Beauty revealed
Over life anew.

There is a spring
One's feet energised
Talking and laughing
Recollecting the partying
Faces smiling
A great feast
Its aroma enticing

The studious days ease
To settling down
Relaxed to begin
A life at 40
Of friends and wine
And places to visit
Wrinkles o-proud
No boundaries unheeded.

Dr Ross Cooper

HOW DARE THE SPRING?

how dare the daffodils
litter the lawns and fields and hedges
in their lovely gold profusion
and the Co-op polyanthus flaunt
their gaudy oranges and purple blooms
and the birds warble and whistle
quarrelling and mating
as though tomorrow is another day
and the pink sunset evenings offer invitations
of summertime
how dare the grass grow
moss thick
and the trees sweep into blossom
into bud into leaf
as thought nothing whatever has happened
how dare the spring?

I stand alone in my outrage
the long warm days
the subject of jubilation –
I stand like some misplaced harridan of doom
cursing in beds of primrose
shrieking and weeping at the wide blue sky
across which I write
don't you know – he's dead
but a high white cloud
dances across the message and
as thought nothing of import has happened
the world turns
how dare the spring?

Penny Anne Windsor

MID-LIFE CRISIS

Seven year itch knocking at my door,
making me twitch, always looking round for more.
Reaction, passion, antidote to boredom,
chained by obligations, duty and then some.
Day after day the same old grind,
slowly chipping holes and worries in my mind.
Responsible, conventional, things I never thought,
ruling my life with words like 'should' and 'ought'.

The fire in my belly tempered steel by time,
the loving in my heart refined until it shines.
I know now what I don't want, learned the hard way round,
but something deep inside me is still waiting to be found.
Drunken nights, danced till dawn,
spontaneous thoughts from freedom born.
All lost in the mire of life's wheel turning,
the embers are low, can't keep the fire burning.

Meditation, religion, the wisdom of age,
sometimes I feel I'm not on the same page.
Searching for something to make me feel alive,
looking for an extra thrill to boost my old hard drive.
Moments of precious time delicate as glass
holding tight to memories as the years fly past.
I'm looking for a spark, a rekindling of the soul,
something true to fill the void and not just plug the hole.

Julie Coomer

OUR WORLD

The world is in a turmoil
Fighting here and fighting there
The world is in a turmoil
Fighting everywhere

You have got something we want
We will fight until we get it
Then impose our rules on you
And you'll not forget it

From time immemorial
It has always been the same
The pages of history tell us so
Most countries share the blame

There was Attila the Hun
And Genghis Khan who led the Mongol hordes
The Saxons, the Vikings, the Romans
And the Norman Overlords

There were two world wars
To end all wars
But still the fighting goes on
The middle east, the far east
And places closer to home

There is wrecking and looting, pillaging, burning
Leaving the people traumatized
To see their life's work destroyed in a flash
And we are supposed to be civilised.

Joyce Cunning

BURN THE HOUSE DOWN

A short sleeved rolled up gingham hipster's
Wistful glazy eyes gaze, hypnotised,
Into a sparkling stretch of water.
Flattened golden grass mirrors blades of hay,
Mutating the scene to olde skool sweet sixteen
Visions of Huckleberry Finn in torn jeans.
Digging the babes soaking up the rays,
He drinks from the elixir of adolescence;
Savouring the essence of the summer of '89 . . .

Detroit house spins like a Kansas City whirlwind through concrete inner city hoods.
Big Fun smiley T-shirts shine on paving slabs in the square,
Warm Roland 303 analogue vibes permeate the air;
Foreshadowing a chemical beat explosion of the future.

Ghettos blast the house down.
Higher state mixes trip in the sun's mushrooming beam,
Adored by fervent disciples practising the art of LSD meltdown.

Deep Heat tracks join the polka dots together;
Mapping out the grooves of a feral youth generation
Whose arms sway in spazzed out trails,
Jacking to the Sound of the Underground.
The Snowball mix intro of *Humanoid* burns acid singed hearts,
Ascending to its volcanic eruption into schizophrenic digitized mayhem.

Teenagers toss Schlitz and Red Stripe down their throats,
Slagging off the Wan Can Dans who cannae handle the buzz.
Jolly Roger delivers his *Acid Man* mantra sermon,
Preaching above squelchy bass and high frequency bleeps
Whilst the tabloids screech in puritanical horror
– A different kinda Sun warning of the spaced out danger;
But parental heads cower sheepishly at the alarm,
Recalling their own hallucinogenic kool counterculture.

Let me take you to a place I know you wanna go, it's a good life
Butterflies above a hard industrial house sound,
A funky dreaded rapper spits his rhymes to a chugging
Boom chick-a chick (heyyy, oooh)
Chick-a chick (heyyy, oooh).
Girl I'll house you,
Girl I'll house you,
Girl I'll house you,
Pumps with the strobes and sirens;
Teasing dreams of desire.
Passion stokes fiery hormones fantasising of long steamy kisses

With the girls traversing the span of a hazy dual carriageway,
Beyond the gauntlet of a hydrant ejaculating Niagara Falls in reverse.

Paris Grey,
Kevin Saunderson,
Todd Terry,
Jazzie B and Soul II Soul,
British Knights,
Troop trainers;
Reel off the tongue
Like items on 1989's Generation Game.

. . . Rewind back to our Huckleberry sucking on sprigs of straw,
Dangling his legs into water glistening like rubies.
Blissfully oblivious of the *Ride on Time* monster,
His toes dance with the fish pirouetting in serenity;
In the canal flowing into the dear emerald city.

Jason Golaup

STAND WITH ME

Follow me my brothers and show no fear,
Stand fast, take the hit, don't shed a tear.
Make fathers proud and mothers weep,
As all before us we shall sweep.

Fear no pain and don't look back,
Press forward, do not change your tack.
Until your foe cries out for quarter,
And seeks to flee from the slaughter.

Turn muscle to iron, steel your hearts,
We shall all be required to play our parts.
I do not ask you to step where I dare not,
Nor do I ask you to follow like a mindless flock.

Instead I say we stand together,
Upon this day we live forever,
So step forward brothers and onto glory,
Let us seize this chance to etch our story.

Jonathan Banks

THE GIRL WHO SHARED MY BED

This is to the girl who shared my bed.
Measuring five foot eleven. Red Hair. Gorgeous legs.

This is to the girl who shared my bed.
From Ireland born and bred,
you said you weren't ready yet
so we didn't have sex, we just slept,
a sequence of events which, in retrospect, was for the best,
especially considering what happened next.

This is to the girl who shared my bed.
Why was it so awkward in the morning when you left?
You didn't stay for breakfast,
simply gathered up your clothes which on my bedroom floor were spread,
picked up your bag, shuddered a goodbye,
and went.

This is to the girl who shared my bed.
Why did you avoid me for weeks after the event,
and when we eventually met again,
avoid any discussion of the subject?

This is to the girl who shared my bed.
I understand and I respect
that you probably just wanted my feelings spared,
because you know as well as anybody knows
that nobody likes to feel an object of regret,
so I'm not accusing you of any malicious intent.

This is to the girl who shared my bed.
But to tell the truth I wish you could've said
something to me, because honesty is the best policy
and honestly –
you were putting me through hell those weeks
when you were always in my head,
and I was evidently not in yours;
now this is all in hindsight, of course,
but if we'd have talked, and I'd have got some closure
I could've had most of the pain over and done with much more suddenly
instead of spending those weeks in uncertainty wondering
and wondering and wondering
if you might come back and love me.

This is to the girl who shared my bed.
Was it something in the way I wrapped my arms around your breasts?
Was it something in the way my nervous breath
brushed warm and uneven against the back of your neck
that made you think I couldn't be a friend?

This is to the girl who shared my bed.
Or was it all because of that poetry I read to you before we slept,
which made you think that I was maybe
a bit gone in the head?
I think it was Coleridge's *Kubla Khan,* but I forget,
although I remember very clearly that instead
of drinking the delicious milk of Paradise
something in you simply cried, 'Beware! Beware!'
and then the next day you hastily got up and left
my pleading eyes, my sweaty hair.

This is to the girl who shared my bed.
I want you to know
that I only wanted to show you in the poetry
something that was truly precious to me,
in the hope that you'd see the connection between
my act of showing something I considered precious to you,
and my overwhelming feeling that you
were something I considered precious too.

This is to the girl who shared my bed.
Although perhaps you knew exactly what the poem meant.
Maybe the feelings which to you I did present
were too intimidating in their strength.

This is to the girl who shared my bed.
none of this really matters anymore I guess,
and I ought to stress I feel no animosity towards that girl
who measures five-eleven,
whose hair is red,
who's got those gorgeous legs
from Ireland born and bred.
I've only got one question for her left,
which up 'til now has on my heart alone been heavy pressed.

So this is to the girl who shared my bed.
Why was it that throughout the time
I needed someone
to reach out and help me feel a little more alive,
you acted as if I was dead?

Bradley Ford

SCHOOL PICK UP

Hustling, bustling, chaotic streams
Bobbing heads bursting with life
Expectant eyes searching the waiting seams
Rich veined with granddads and grannies, uncles and aunties
Brothers and mothers, dawdling daddies
Sisters and cousins and whatnots
A myriad sea, eldered humanity
Smiling, frowning
Being

A roll call of little names
I can't see! I can't see!
Who's here to collect me?
Sarah's gone, Amy too
But where . . .
    Where is the someone for me?

Moved to the side
Unexpectedly
Little minds wonder their fate
Maybe they're late
Maybe they've forgotten me
Maybe they're not coming
Maybe I've been left
Forever left . . .

Emily said I was her friend
Her bestest friend
That's what she said
Emily's my friend too
And Sarah and Amy
Although they've both gone
Emily's just behind talking to Dylan

Oh, there they are!
I thought you were never coming
I can't wait to tell you all the things
Of colouring and making and doing
Stories about aliens in underpants
And walking to the moon
A giant balloon made of blankets

And . . .
    And . . .
        And . . .
            Lots of other stuff too!

Your hand feels warm and safe; Emily's waving
She's my bestest friend, you know
Bye Emily, see you tomorrow!

Mark Dorey

LYRICS

A bit like lyrics.
Raw, rebellious, razor-sharp rhyming,
rhythm polished to imperfect perfection,
blindingly bright shined
and breathed into being,
bringing green-leafed questions into our vibrant horizon

Placing star-gazing, daydreaming, people-watching
on a plate.
We – more colourful than any spectrum,
more powerful than fate,
train pupils to *see,*
persuade souls to soar, free.

A bit like lyrics.
Undressed metrics.
Where in-your-face and beyond-the-surface
intricately intertwine.
Where complexity and simplicity unfold and combine.
Where verbal acrobatics are free-styled like
weekend time unwind.
Dancing between the lines of
shadow and lime.
Drunk on poetic chemicals,
the red, red wine of loose rhyme.

A little bit lyrical.
A bit metrical.
A bit rhythmical.
Maybe . . . a metaphysical miracle?
Or maybe . . . *for the people.*
Speaking bass-less music
to unsung heroes.
Feel the unseen parade beating on your eardrum.
This poetry's for you.
Just another form of a song of freedom.

Claudia MacCarthy

NATURE'S CORNER

The first light of morning gradually peeps through the window
It heralds the light of another new day.
The autumn wind sighs through the trees in the garden
And dew on the branches looks like diamonds I'd say.
How those raindrops glitter and glisten at twilight.
As they shine on dull November's first light.
And the rising sun shines like gold in the morning
Against the red sky, that's ever so bright.
And those grey rain clouds hover around the horizon
And the mist like a cold shroud in the air it will cling.
Yet in every dark cloud there's a bright silver lining.
Soon the November sunshine will brighten the sky
Remaining leaves on the trees by the roadside,
Fall like sovereigns of gold on the ground.
Followed by seeds of every size and description.
As they're sown by nature's great sower, the wind.
It scatters them right across meadows and woodlands,
And any place where fertile soil can be found.
in the seed bed of Earth, the great garden of nature
that we see as unpleasant, cold, wet, rain-soaked ground.
It's hard to imagine that days were much warmer.
Yes, days that were longer, and times spent in the sun
But just like night as it transforms into morning
The seasons will change, the go, and they come.

James McIlhatton

WARMTH

It's hot as the sun, reflects its beams into the Earth.

But there's a warmth really hotter than those, where I found myself hot, it's in your arms . . .

Protection they mean for me, safety in another words, reassurance of the perfect day that tomorrow will bring.
Those hot beams reflect in my eyes when I wake up, but they'll never be warmer than your arms, than your body.
I don't mind to lose myself in that hot desert as long as it keeps me warm, I won't need a sunlight to show me a path, to show me way, your desert gives the map to the 'promised place', which is your mind, and that's the warmest place I can get to when the cold is trying to catch me.

Jorge Monteiro

THE BLACKBIRD

A veritable pocket-rocket, jet-black thrush
Ever on a quest, always at a rush
Bird of the verge, garden and hedge
Ever nervous, always on edge
Inspecting its domain, guarding it with zeal
Ever cautious, always its threats real
An unlicensed shadow cloaked in black
Ever restless, always changing tack
Pulsating without a pause, so twitchy
Every skittish, always so jittery
Light-footed, bounding on scaly claws
Ever nimble, always with a cause
Mischievous clockwork toy ticking
Ever hungry, always a worm needs picking
Ambush set square, primed to pounce
Ever dagger-ready, always unannounced
Jabs turn into forceps with morsel held in beak
Ever scouting for more, always held oblique
Reptilian riposte, ratcheted on a spring
Ever tenacious, always scurrying
Rising and dropping in carousellic blur
Ever highly-charged, always on a spur
My feathered friend, eyes bulbous bright
Ever watchful, always beset with fright
An avian cipher, scampering in the brush
Ever so secretive, always in a hush
When in a fluster, whimpers out a wheeze
Ever diving for cover, always hides in trees
My blackbird, a roving sentinel of its realm
Ever unnoticed, always so sneaky at the helm

Alex Newman

DEAR DAD

Aged 9
Dear Daddy,
I know you and Mummy had a paddy.
I hope you don't stay away too long,
Can't you just call Mummy and say sorry for what you did wrong?
You see Daddy, that's why I'm writing this letter,
To help you think of a way to make things better.
Why don't you buy flowers or send a rose?
I know that you love us, just make sure Mum knows.
Please find a way to make things okay,
I miss you more than this letter can say.
I still love you, all the sugar in the world,
Come home soon –

Your little girl.

Aged 13
Dear *Dad,*
Even writing that word makes me mad!
You should know it's uttered in a disinterested moan,
Written in italics with a sarcastic undertone.
Well thanks for coming back. Oh no wait, you didn't come,
You only ever said hello and then asked to speak to Mum.
I can only presume that you got bored of doing the fatherly stuff that you oughta,
Which is probably why you walked out on your wife and two young daughters,
It's funny really – you wanted to leave your kids and wife,
But then walked into exactly the same life.
Well here you go Dad! This is really all I've got!
Sincerely –

The daughter you forgot.

Aged 16
To whom it may concern,
Sorry if that opener leaves a slight burn,
But it hardly seems appropriate to call you Dad anymore –
Personally I think that name went along with you when you walked out the door.
So how is the new family? All well I hope.
I can only pray that this time you find it easier to cope.
You know, sometimes I replay when you left, over and over again –
I suspect it's the root cause of my issues with men.
People seem to think I'm looking for a father figure just like you,
Although I don't know why I'd bother after all you put me through.
It's a pity you weren't around, but you always could be a bit of a no-show.
Many thanks –
From the girl you used to know.

Aged 19
I don't want an overly bitter or too-formal start
But calling you Dad causes conflict in my heart
So maybe I should leave the Dear Sir part blank.
I'm not writing to be nasty or to hurl abuse
Because after a decade I figured, hey, what's the use?
You've missed out on a lot – I don't know how much you know,
But I've decided to try my hand at poetry shows
Although, between you and I, I'm not sure how well that's going.
It's amazing how much I've changed without you even knowing.
So I live in Bristol now, and I'm at university,
I study English Language but my heart still belongs to poetry,
As you can see.
And I'm finally over you leaving, I'm not angry or sad,
Because it turns out Mum was also a pretty good dad.
So I'll stop the snide comments and let go of the rage,
Mostly to try and stop if from infiltrating every page of my notebook.
It's a shame things didn't turn out how we all thought they'd be,
Although you did make us all stronger as a family
And that consolation feels better than any first prize to me.
I hope this letter gets there safely –

Sincerely, Charley.

Charlotte Barnes

UNTITLED

At long last the clouds move south
And that plasma ball shouts from its mouth
Weighing down the stratosphere
On top of the troposphere
And we gasp at hot air
But we don't really care
Insects get drunk on rotting fruit
And buzz around with one boot
Our arms all shades of red
But we'll soak it up until the sun goes to bed

Heather Cooke

SOMETIMES

Sometimes only a horse will do.
When you need the best of friends,
No questions asked,
Who understands without words,
You want someone bigger than you,
Who is there when you need.

When the best daddy in the world
Is no longer able to hug you,
No talking can help,
A big neck, silent understanding,
No hurry, nowhere else to be.
A horse has total empathy.

Sometimes only a horse will do.
You want to scream and cry,
But must not do.
Go to the paddock fence and call,
Fling your arms around the neck,
Sob as long as you need.

Your dog wants to lick you better,
Your family to talk it through.
A horse will understand,
Will heal your troubles and woes,
Bring inner peace and calmness,
Be there when you need him to,

Because,

Sometimes only a horse will do.

Ingrid Knight

HOUSEWORK BLUES

My heart sinks as I do the washing up.
My soul drains as I reach for the tea towel.
The vacuuming sucks the life out of me
And the ironing leaves me feeling flat.
My luster lessens as I polish
And as I buff the mirror I reflect on my lot.
Wishing I could be swept off my feet
I head for the broom cupboard
And wonder if I should brush up on my act.
Feeling fat as I plump the cushions.
I thirst for more as I water the plants.
Feeling strung out as I hang the washing,
My heart is on the line.
My dreams go up in smoke as I light the fire
I darn the socks and feel that I am losing the thread.

Caroline Peacock

REALITY

Dulce et Decorum . . .
Honour. Honourable to die when cowering in fear?
Fight. Fighting for survival when the end seems so near
Die. Dying – Inevitable! And it scares us to the core
Country. Country of hell if we lose this war
Fearing the endless inevitable hell
Our only survival; the stories you tell
Out here men are broken:
Because we are scared, we are shamed
Men in reality:
Poisoned and pained
This is the real men, this is their story
All this? All this is for
Pro Patria Mori

Layla Claridge

GLEISION

They were born with coal;
black, hard unfeeling.
Four more ghosts
in orange boiler suits,
walk the world tonight.
The blackened faces
searching for the homes
that they can no longer find.
The tears in the valley trickle
like autumn rains down the faces
of those that are left behind.
The tributes from the great and good
clang with a hollow lack of understanding.
What would they know of tragedy?
Chipping Norton is a long way
from the mine filled with water;
and the bloated hirsute faces of drowned men.
The day after tomorrow, the world
will move on, and it will forget.
The wives, the mothers and the children
stand alone in the street.
And look at the mine
that stole their hopes away.

Wayne Whiskerd

QUESTION TIME AT 2AM

Shadows, injured bedsprings and the full moon
Bobbing through backlit clouds like a balloon
Retreat as you unfold from your cocoon:
Uncoupling from my finger hook your womb
You stretch as if you're measuring the room,
Lazarus with boobs arising from the tomb,
Standing there as undead as the crossed hairs
Etched in the sniper's sight still atticked upstairs
With other junk from Daddy's Cold War years,
And ask, as you've maybe asked your previous guys,
'How come you never look into my eyes
When performing press-ups between my thighs?'

A D Harvey

THE FUTURE OF THE WIND

They stole the Earth, they stole the clay
Once just for pots, but now today
To mould hi-tec ceramic tools;
From levels deep beneath the soil
They stole the coal and then the oil,
The godlike power in molecules
They stole for carcinogenic fuels
That made our babies' flesh decay;
The water they stole too so they
Could cool or heat their factories,
They stole the grass, they stole the trees
And now they want to steal the breeze
With huge propellers on the hills
The future's 'bright swastikic mills'.

Ping Zheng

STRENGTH THROUGH COURAGE

Bellowing, silver mosquitoes
So close; hear the pistons sing
The buzzing, ringing, banging sound
Is less powerful than its sting.

Men piled like boys' toys
Green figures fall
You shout and cry: there's no help now
You're just a distant call

Wishing you had just one wish:
To live your life once more
Thinking of a wife at home
You lie helpless on the floor

Those heroes shall be remembered
Their victory in Britain's song
As all the blood lost in the war is keeping Britain strong.

Katie Lawless

GONE AWAY

Dear Mother, can you hear me moving?
It has been six whole weeks
since I have left your home

Still, in it, this wasteland
I am, I am
It is feeling like my home

Memo to self:
Memorise Rubbish Collection Schedule
I forgot
Pay attention to the details
I forgot
Remember: do not waste any time

Dear Mother, can you hear me laughing?
It has been eighteen whole weeks
Since I have left your home

Never, ever leaving it, this wasteland
I am, I am
All I own is here, inside

Things to buy:
Do not forget to buy electricity
Internet
Electrical appliances
Internet
Till then, all I need is there, outside

Dear Mother, can you hear me crying?
It has been nine whole months
Since I have left your home

Never, ever visiting it, this paradise
Not yet, not now
Dear Mother, I am here, down here

To do:
Dry whining eyes
Everything
More, Dear Mother
Everything
Pay attention: do not waste time

Susannah Makram

AS I WALKED

As I walked
You came to me
A warm wind
Enveloping my
Hopelessness,
I felt your arms
My mother
Nestling my
Loneliness
Knowing that you
Had once stood
Where I was
Standing now

Facing the rock-face
Between terminal
Despair
And the unknown
Being that vast
Drop into
Darkness of
Unimaginable things and
Places to
Resurface who
Knows where.

R O'Connor-D'Andel

WE ARE SELFISH

Locked alone in a frenzied place.
Desperation would not cease. Busy nurses could not check.
Collapsible rail did not break.
Alarms. Surprises.
'She's not breathing,' yelled in panic.

Much too young; a tragedy.
I know why; I know too much.

You.
Me.

Sick.

Liz Stephens

RICHMOND PARK

We are in Richmond Park.
Your cousin shaving your five-year-old hair
And a kebab from Clock House Grill at 12.57am.

Westfield in the sun
With a cinnamon sugar pretzel that left three pounds sitting in our pockets.
Then knotty bricks catch between our legs as we sit on the wall off Chaffinch Road.

I am size four blisters –
Unacceptable photographs, an uncontrollable laugh
That glued my eyes to my cheeks . . .
And then it's crazy that it's only been a week.

Hooks and claws and security door licenses,
And a guy that 'went in' at the post office.
Collar up and blue toothed ears, albino deer, a bike with no gears.
Chillin' with the mandem,
Can dem not feel our eyes on her hand on his thigh?

You are the popcorn stuck to my top at the back of the cinema
And going to the toilet with one shoe on.
A blue GameBoy Advance your dad bought you that naivety stole
And a sandy bird in your desk
4,000 miles west and twelve years back from where we stand.
I am calling cats that don't speak my language and my palms clasped around your stomach.

Breaking school world records as we cycle on tarmac.
Just doing what we do
Like we knew this was where we were supposed to be.

It's not knowing your limits,
Not giving a single damn about them
And getting soaked in your work uniform.

'Stamina-less drunk' and Prince B's flyer,
a punctured tyre repaired by a guy who told us too late about the cheaper café down the road.
Kids dragging logs into pondweed for penguins to skate on and
Finding waterfall in places they don't belong,
Like us.

Spitting out water on the 27th of July after my white shirt turned
Transparent
And your hands went up my back.

Then it all got too much
And laughing became easy,
Talking became easy
Happy became so easy.

Mango and lime at Nandos with five free stamps is ours
And BBQ based pizza from Dominos.
You just don't know but it became too easy

But I wasn't free to be dreaming of you –
Someone who fasts and takes me home after dark
Sits down with me on benches in Richmond Park.

Knows what I'm saying when I say it.
Don't play games and takes a break when I need it.
Makes a list of places to go from calendars . . .
And that's just his thing.

And all the things he won't do
You do them with ease
And we don't want to do things in routine.

Only time to sleep is the weekend but even then he still leaves at 11.

But I wasn't free to be dreaming of you –
Someone who fasts and takes me home after dark
Sits down with me on benches in Richmond Park.
Knows what I'm saying when I say it.
Don't play games and takes a break when I need it.
Makes a list of places to go from calendars . . .
And that's just his thing.

Cleo Asabre-Holt

PRE·SENSE

An angel's presence
makes fear vanish,
makes up for lover's wish,
embraces you in its essence.
Glorious in your light
from within
Which shines inside-out
and lets you be.
Dearest carers whose love has taken over
Angel's presence;
befriends and awakens

Elizabeth Lorena Faitarone

DESECRATION

(Dedicated to Camilla Carr and her Partner John James who were taken hostage by Chechnian rebels, in 1997. Their ordeal lasted 14 months)

'Herpes . . . No sex . . . No violence . . . ' I said
Repeating my magical mantra
I'm not my body, I think to myself in my head

In his dreams my boyfriend murders the gangster
For he raped me over and over again
Trembling, I repeat my magical mantra

It was all I could do to keep sane
My captor held me down and he
Raped me over and over again

And yet in my agony he could not see
Nor touch the essence inside of me
My Jailor held me down and then he

Desecrated my humanity
Yet something in me remained calm
He could not disturb the silence in me

I knew then I could come to no harm
For there is something in me always free
And this something always remains calm
Then I think to myself in my head: *you are forgiven.*

Michael Smith

UNTITLED

Your mother's always said you need more calcium, so your bones are strong
And you don't find yourself middle-aged in a concrete stairwell with you
Skeleton snapped in two because it just couldn't withstand the fact
You don't like milk. So you learn their names and sang to the tune of
Mandible, occipital, frontal, parietal, partial to the abrasive
Cut against your *incisor, canine, premolar* bloodstained
Mint-green mark on the porcelain, crack through the *lunate*
Capitate, hamate, trapezoid, swelling to mutation on the
left side.
But your mother doesn't know the slack-jawed snap
of patella, femur, phalanx, carpal, she only knows
their textbook sheen, the ways they'd bleed from her mouth in dull
ink. Your mother's missing the point; the way you choke down
lactose makes your stomach freeze over, dulls the dizzying dental
crunch of radius, tibia, fibular, ulna, that wings and ruptures astutely
through your sternum, manubrium, thoracic following the xyphoid
process from that piss-stained heap at the foot of the stairs and
holds your head under your armoury of words so you might really know the meaning
of a calcium deficiency and an emotional stutter having never broken a bone,
never stumbled on an 'I love you', never choked on an apology
with the taste of full fat in the back of your throat.

One day you come home and your mother's sat at the table, waiting for you,
with a glass of cold milk in her hands.

Jasmine Hide

FIVE STEPS TO WELLBEING

Five steps to wellbeing is what they say,
To keep me active in every way.
Connect with family and friends abroad,
Skyping my grandkids is my reward.
Paying my bills and shopping online,
Sharpens my skills as well as my mind.

Exercise they say, it makes you feel good,
Although I am reluctant, I know that I should.
Running and weight-lifting is not what I am needing
But simply a walk or maybe some weeding.
A dance with some friends at our local hall,
Is much more my level and fun for all.

Take notice of the world, it's so appealing,
Be curious of life and how I am feeling.
They say enjoy it no matter the weather,
Savour the moments, as we're not here forever.

It's never too late to learn something new,
To take up a skill or a hobby or two.
I'll paint a picture or write a book,
Or maybe it's time I learnt how to cook.
There is so much out there for me to uncover,
To find myself and rediscover.

Now that I know what I can achieve,
I want to give back before I leave.
I know now that I have nothing to fear,
I'll give my time and volunteer.
I'll help someone else and show them the way,
Five steps of wellbeing is what I'll say.

Claire Dobson

FOR A FRIEND

I can't see you but I know you're here,
My dear, best friend of two and a half years.
My one constant in my life
You gave me love, perspective
And purpose through all the strife
One day I'm fine
The next I'm not
The grief I've got
Just doesn't go away
You're in my heart,
Forever with me you stay.
I can't see you but I know
You're near,
No, you're here
In my heart, my head
In my house, on my bed
In the backyard and in the sun
My friend, my love, my special
Special one,
I know it was your time to go,
But oh how I wish it wasn't so
Just to have one last cuddle
I would give anything
That's all I can say.
Rest easy my friend, wherever you are
From my mind you're never far
Now I can see
I know you're here
My dear, best friend of two and a half years.

Frances Fulcher

MEMORIES

We walked on Lakeland's leafy dales
On Cornwall's sandy shore
On Cotswold stone we rested
And tramped on Devon moors
The mist was grey on Dartmoor
The wind blew on the Clee
The magic of Welsh mountains
Still calls to you and me
We whispered under Cheddar
We swam in oceans blue
The rain was cool in Newlyn
The sand was warm in Looe
We laughed and loved in Keswick
The tigers roared in Kent
I treasure every moment
Of togetherness we spent
Hands held we climbed up Malvern
We drove on Roman road
And in the streets of our home town
We shared the worry load
Our love grew in the woodlands
It blossomed by the streams
It nearly died one autumn
Saved only by our dreams
In Leamington we lost a life
In London town we cried
In Birmingham I lost you once
That time you nearly died
Oldswinford gave a new life
In Clent the bluebells grew
At Island pool the poppy field
Church Stretton held the view
The peacocks called At Warwick
A robin at Grasmere
We made friends with the finches
Not far from Windermere
We stood where Drake had lingered
Where seagulls swoop and call
And on the cliffs at Dover
You held me lest I fall
We watched the carp at Chartwell
The same fish Churchill knew
At Bladen where they laid him
We spent an hour or two

The marvels on Goonhilly
The sadness at Land's End
The harbour at Portscatho
We found a furry friend
This dear beloved country
Has treasures by the score
We found a few together
The years hold many more.

Thelma O Brookes

CLOUD NINE

Life on cloud nine
The weather is looking fine
Trees are blowing in the breeze
Birds are singing as they please
The sun has started to rise
Here come the bees and the butterflies
Looking for nectar they rest on a flower
They get to work with their magical powers.

On cloud nine
The sun continues to shine
Living creatures roam throughout the day
Other creatures are kept hidden away
The running rivers and quiet streams
Are so surreal and so supreme
As darkness comes and now it's night
More wildlife tends to come into sight.

On cloud nine
Seasons change with time
The months and years go by
New life is born and the old will die
The world will keep on turning
The fire will stay burning
Living an existence on cloud nine
Will eventually appeal to all Mankind.

Lynsey Harris

DARK SHADOWS

There's an emptiness
Deep inside me
Feels like a hole
Where feelings of love should be
Were the feelings ever there
or was my heart always this way?
Feels like an emptiness that's here to stay
Waiting
For my heart to slowly decay
Every day
I wake up with a numbness to my soul
Waiting for something to change me
Make me complete
Make me normal
I drift along day by day
Wondering how I came to be this way
No one understands me
No one really cares
Just empty people
With empty stares.

Rehnaaz Dodya

THE MERCY JOURNEY

My journey began at dawn.
The following day, my journey began.
How bizarre were my dreams,
And what silence explained,
The hope beyond the setting sun.

'Tis mystery all! 'What causes this?' I cried.
Surely the first dawn spoke untrue.
My mind was perplexed,
My mind was tormented,
And if you caused it, I blame you!

Oh Jesus! What a night!
Where all my blackness was rent.
But love came in;
The second dawn,
And that mercy was Heaven sent!

Nicholas John Sweetland

A COMPLEX TUNE

My heart composes the sounds,
My mind lays them out and then conducts,
My hands wave the batons like wands,
And like magic, music is struck!
Sometimes it is ruthless and rough
Sometimes it is rootless and fucked,
But most of the time when I combine these chimes,
What I hear is beautiful stuff,
A symphony is my life story,
A complex tune with highs and lows,
Fear has brass instruments come crashing down,
Eagerness sets the drums out on a roll,
I feel bold and brave when the guitar's strings are struck,
I feel safe when the mighty horn has been sound,
And the sweet whistle from the flutes helps to lift me up when down,
The tambourine is for dancing feet,
The xylophone helps them potter along,
But whatever my inner orchestra decides to play . . .
I'm the one conducting the song!

Robert Kelly

A STRANGE OCCURRENCE . . .

I was flying in a spaceship, traveling fast far out in space,
And we landed on a planet, where the people were of a strange race,
They had bald pointed heads and sunken eyes,
And their bodies, were small and thin,
They uttered no words, but certainly knew
What thoughts of mine lay within,
I wasn't frightened, I wasn't scared,
Just completely at my ease,
They seemed to want to examine me
From my head down to my knees,
No surgery, no injections, no drugs were used at all
Just the feel of gentle fingers, probing my body parts overall,
Did I just dream about this flight?
Did it happen, or was it something I had read?

Dave Cole

WE SHALL SEE

We breathe,
both at ease
As the whistling wind
blows to a whisper.
We beam
under moon's shadow
Lit by flickering street lamps along arcades ring shrills of good fortune.

We sit
On our lap
With a newspaper-wrapped
portion of chips
We kiss with salty lips
Flapping and smacking against each other, like a blanket in the breeze.

We flop
upon each other
Like seaweed on a rock.
A boat docks
We listen . . .
to melodies from seas
and sailors mumble, fondle sand, like a wandering hand up my skirt.

We wriggle
Snorkelling and searching
Intently riding waves
Wandering back and forth
We dally
towards each other, dive and swim like blurring blue ink merging with paper.

We fold
a pebble pulled
from the ground
Instead of skipping along
We'd slipped
each other's grip
Fell open, like pages from a book the current took and divided.

I ached
Searching everywhere
But he was lost.
Waiting to be found
I hoped
the ocean would dilute my pain, and washed up I'd find us cuddling again.

Nicky Archer

OWN UP

I've been there. I've done that. I'll go there,
no more. Now I come, to settle the score.
No matter what, this stays true, never do
unto others, what you wouldn't like for you.
'Cause when the tables fall down it will harm you.

You say you're a bad boy who's on the run?
If you did good own up to what you done.
so you built your empire on other people's
grief and act like you have something to
teach. When every word in your speech
Is contrary to what you preach.

You read the paper and for a brief think
You're a gangster. You're a bully and a thief you
killer, coward! Practise what you preach. I'm not the one
with a blade, or a gun, but I know what you've done
to someone's mother, brother, sister, son . . .
The list goes on.

Now they call me an informer. When the fact of
the matter is I couldn't turn a blind eye. I talked to
the Po Po, I didn't deny, I stood for truth. You stooped
to lies now that boy is taking innocent guys.
I would have seen justice but that fell through.

He's free to do whatever he wants to.
Breaking news is through, he's
wanted for a murder. I blame you and you, and you.
when there was a chance to put him away
you chose to play safe.

Nephew, daddy uncle gone! All because
I didn't want to be the one, so I turned
face at what was going on. He feels unstoppable,
on a power trip having fun. For the heck of it
up to your neck in it.
Hangman you're gone.

Natasha Harris

THAMES NIGHT

Night was warm and sultry
Low tide smelt pungent strong
River life began to muster
Awaiting late moon song
Birds ducks swans and geese
Herons, cormorants, parakeets
All sleeping in the trees
Or far from foxes' conceit
Voles and rats and all things small
Woke up to live the dark
Scurrying here and there about
Badgers foxes quietly barked
Moonlight seeped from behind the clouds
Showing a ghostly scene
Where life took pace in slow motion
Like sketch of day-dwellers' dream
Mr Fox searched out a careless duck
He swallowed it without a scream
Barn owl scoured and quickly spied
Water vole's tiny sheen
He dived and missed went up again
Many more to hunt tonight
Bats swooped and fluttered turning fast
Catching insects and grubs in flight
There was commotion on Chiswick Bridge
Two figures struggling hard
One strong pushed arms flailing fast
Hit shallow mud and jarred
Neck broken
Body all limp as life departed
Death took over the corpse
A hint of ghost appeared in the shallows
It appeared to be pulling it ashore
With the help of the flow of the current
The cadaver slunk into weeds
Well caught there it rested all hidden
Tended by its spirit freed
Time passed till searchlights scoured the Thames
Helicopter combing the shores
Lifeboat roared round the bend all flares
Activity bustled galore
Our lady lay serene and slack
Her golden hair surround
Ghost cradled her to hide her view

Search party to confound
Dawn was breaking grey at first
Then slashes of pink and red
Like knife wounds cut into the sky
Of another's murdered dead
Now seabirds rise and circle high
Come up from bad weather coast
River moves with life of day
Ignoring the corpse exposed
This stays caught up in reeds and such
Awaiting an extra tide
Then surely its journey down to the deep
Would take a turn outside
Herons fish and cormorants dive
Geese shepherd their young upstream
Life that is just carries on
Another daytime dream.

Vicki Naylor

SHUTDOWN

Depressed
All messed up, again
My head, won't let me get
Out of bed, again
Sweat and pains
running, down my body like heavy rain
I'm drowning again.
Agitated, manipulated,
Deteriorated, again
Desperate to obliterate
Block out air
Consumed by darkness
Despair
Close the door
Get down on the floor
Can't take anymore, again.

Mandy Younger

SHAFTS OF LIGHT

Dawn heralded by light beyond darkness
Increasingly pervaded the misty stillness
Of a late summer morning
A world held captive by the luxury –
Shafts of red and gold
Warm humid day to follow
Pleasant stroll amidst the forest trees
Swathed and bathed in light filtered to spectral purity
Shafts reciprocating skywards
sometimes Summertime's sensations
Dark upon light, light's bolts from the blue
– strange term – usual, ominous, dark hue
Light from dark, ferocious in its intensity
Thunderous applause from innocent bystanders
Serenity's great equalizer
To light again from lit up blackness of the heavens
A catharsis for emotive balance
Dusk fell and the day thou gavest
Supplanted by dreams dancing on the moonbeams.

William Graham

FIRST LAMB

The ewe has stretched her pain upon the straw,
Unsure now of what, so strong, exerts its pull
On her. A sudden rush of thin, soaked wool.
And here, lying for dead, upon the floor,
The lamb. Now she that could give no more
In cramped space, or elapsed days, she was that full
Of birth, has fled in fear of this passion cruel
That draws her back to smell this life so raw.
What, this poor gawky thing a sign of grace;
– this bundled collection of spare legs and feet,
struggling on feeble knees gravity to atone?
Look on. The lamb's future is its hope-filled face,
Soft mouth against the ewe's, squeezing its silent bleat
Into her heart, despite the wind's cold moan.

Tom Pyke

WHERE WERE YOU?

Where were you when I needed you most?
In my hour of need nothing, but a ghost
Where were you during those endless hours I cried
During the times when inside I had died?

The promises to always be holding my hand
When in reality alone, again I stand
No one could hear my long lonely screams
Trying to wonder what happened to our dreams.

To hold my hand or kiss me goodnight
Was many memories away, out of sight
To tell me everything was going to work out fine
And reassure me tomorrow the sun would shine

Where were you? You had gone far away
Looking for your own dreams and another day
I stood alone in our forgotten dreams
And forever alone, again it seems

Tomorrow is a brand new day of hopes and fears
To face with bravery and wipe away tears
Together we stood through good and bad
But where are you? Wondering what you had?

Jackie Smith

GLUE

For these few moments,
Wrapped in glue,
I am focused on you.

For these few moments,
Wrapped in glue
I am eclipsed by you.

For these few moments,
Wrapped in glue,
I am haunted by you.

For these few moments,
I'm totally immersed,
In the light of
You . . .

Nick Strong

LOVE POEM

(Written in mind to the up-and-coming piece of art by Janis Stevens entitled 'Love Palm')

The sky so undervalued, a majestic canvas of the world
to portray a simple passing glance of the day or night ahead
With every simple single circle of the globe it changes
to suite the obtuse or acute behaviour of the easy demonstrations
of the weather, whether or not I seem to know where it will go
Come rain or shine, open the curtain I know for certain something will
or won't be there but the paintbrush may portray the obvious
part of the lives today in each effect we look up and we think it will be there.

Whether a daybreak or a midnight hush, whether a ball of gleaming
steaming bright star or a sly sneaky peek of icy fortitude to get you
in an attitude, a silent prose, a frozen fallen rose. A clinger
in the daylight darkness, secret meets and yet a greater part of good
a pool to misbehave in, a floor in which to rave in even a place to hold
a consolation. Or somewhere one could glance and just by chance
see a shooting star, to make a wish come true, only if we knew.

The crimson of awe, the careless descent, the rouge of a cheek
The pink of black cherries floods the sky like rivers flood the Earth
Feed the atmosphere like music feeds our soul, and ignites us with the
ever-changing evergreens the midnight husky blues and the indigo of passion
The golden glow, the classic scarlet, the things we see are briskly mixed
Upon your creative palette of store-bought acrylics. Wonders of the rest which
set alight our hearts with such a wild lair and yet others they do not care.
They will not ever understand such a piece painted by the one.

So stare upon the sky whatever time of day, whatever the weather may be
and then may I ask you start upon the creation of sensational imagination
yet it has the easiest inspiration. The craziest people within us hold
so much dear to our hearts. We may always take for granted the obvious
We never see what is right in front of us and we do judge, every little colour
which flairs brilliantly or not, we shall see that to be passionate,
we can just look up!

Steffi McIntyre

POLITICS OF THE STAFF ROOM

Staff briefing every morning
Five days a week . . .
I look around, staff talking
Laughing, moaning, some are yawning
Head teacher enters without a warning.

Wembley Stadium . . . blah, blah, blah
I think he said something about an event
Some staff rush to move their cars
Blah, blah's baby . . . who's? Awww
Gosh will this day just hurry up and start

The beauty pageant girls walk in
Potential Alpha Males all hush
Silence as the judging begins
Dressed in all the latest things
I wonder who will win?

Alpha Male battle starts
White Shirt makes a joke, Stripy makes another
Everyone including me laughs
Stripy's is better so he get top marks
White Shirt has failed, his poor broken heart

Oh great Mr Charity has something to say
Blah, blah environment, blah, blah, blah
Oh why can't this wait until another day?
An extra sponsorship nobody wants to pay
Can't you raise money another way?

Finally it's eight forty-five, we're all free
Well until tomorrow
No more battles, the winners have been
Staff now have manners and courtesy
Although we're severely stressed and busy bees.

Latoya Maynard

UNTITLED

If, my love, my some fine miracle,
I live to find grey hairs on my head and in
my eyebrows,
and on the fleshy pillowy fingerbacks
then it might not be a testament to our success.

Though I love and though you love
we by equal measures destroy; I killing my urges
to scream when you, with soft tones and sheets try to
bring me to myself, you biting when I deny
you the melancholia that is your nesting place.
I flaunt pretence, we are young and beautiful.
You revel in distress, we are poor and liberal.

Always ascribing a-place-a-point-a-thing to each
flicker of my nostril ,each disjointed climax.
I am. It is enough to say that we exist as proof of possibility
to ache. Your clean hands and eyes next to mine, burnt
and fat, milked of human empathy.
In breaking bread we form a brotherhood,
In breaking beds wee form a parenthood.

If, my love I should die. I *should* die,
and fall into myth; desecrate my plate-washing abilities,
my cooking.
But always say I lived once,
for what is important is the testament to *my* success.

Siobhan Mealey

THE OLD FOLKS' HOME

I sit here left to my own devices,
twiddling the thread from my skirt,
familiar patterns on the carpet looming up to torment me.
It seems I'm just a nobody to be toileted and fed
Oh let them take my dentures and bundle me off to bed.
From the kitchen I hear voices,
I know they're calling out my name,
all the time believing me to be somewhat a little insane.
Play the fool Eliza, play the fool old dear.

Annette Heald

LACRIME D'OCA

The girl that died with a goose by her side,
had never been unpopular, rude or unkind.
The friends she had liked her style,
she even had a boy for a while.
Until the day her father left,
her mother had died from an early death.
The departure of Daddy who'd taught her to fight
– and the difference between wrong and right –
Left the girl in a total mess,
with no one to care for – no one to impress.
She promised herself she'd never repeat the pain,
those torturous days in the rain.
The girl all suffering became a recluse,
her life cold and empty but then came a goose!
Good natured and gorgeous this goose easily found,
the humanity and love she'd dug deep underground.
The tape she'd used to stick herself together,
wasn't needed anymore – a change in the weather.
Others made her nervous but this goose calmed her down,
taught her how to look up and how not to frown.
Step by step the goose changed the girl's existence,
if at first there was any doubt now there was no resistance.
Until the day her father came back home,
joy turned to anger when she saw he wasn't alone.
The goose did all he could but her daddy's latest deception,
saw the girl go back to craving affection.
The goose didn't realise but the hole he'd filled in her heart,
was now under attack – the thread coming apart.
And so despite his best efforts to make the girl smile again,
not to return to that agony – those days in the rain,
After one final hug the goose realised he'd lost his plight,
he wiped a tear from his eye and began his next flight.

Julie D'Adamo

CHANGE

1990 is the date that's engraved
In the copper metal beginning to fade
I belong in a pocket, a till or a jar
But my only company is the cold crumbling tar

In days gone by I'd be exchanged for a sweet
Or collected with others to save for a treat
But times have changed, popularities gone
Now I'm met with a sigh like I've done something wrong

But I'm still used for something, something that spreads
A magic and happiness in childish heads
So in my purse prison I hope to be found
Or lie appealingly on the ground

Once I'm in a pair of excited hands
I'm taken to a well where my wisher stands
He closes his eyes and holds me tight
Then he flips me up and I spin mid-flight

I plummet swiftly from the twenty foot drop
With the wish-giving water I splash to a stop
So I've not been used to buy something new
Instead I've set a wish on its journey to true

Iain Murray

UNTITLED

As a poet I would like to say,
I prefer to do instant poetry,
As I am at that stage in life.
I haven't got a wife.
I can travel anywhere.
To make the audience laugh.
If they concur.
With my opinions.
On what they chose for me.
So I can do instant poetry.
I went to sea to see.
What I could see.
And as expected.
I could see the sea.

Brian Loughborough

DISCOVERY AND EXPLORATION

There's so much to discover,
So much to explore!
What's round that corner?
What's through that door?
Would you like to explore and look under the floor?
Would you like to see castles and forests and more?

If you sit still and stay silent inside,
You'll miss so many things,
So come for a ride!

Let your imagination roam, run, frolic, so freely.
Play games in the sun; visit Gloucester or Ely!
You could go to the beach, or ride on a whale,
Or count all the scales on a catfish's tail!
Why not zoom to the moon,
Or meet a baboon,
Explore a whole jungle or learn a new tune!

There's so much to discover,
So much to explore!
So let's go outside now!
Don't be a bore!

Susannah Foot

PARALLEL ENTROPY OF SYMBIOTIC PARADIGMS

True love does not exist, anguished hearts that cannot feed
There is nothing for us to need, but emotions in the mist.
So we are now what can't be spoken, hidden lies just reveal
That soul and spirit start to feel, what the mind has truly broken.
For one second of this blessing, my life I would gladly give
Ectoplasmic self caressing, what existence cannot forgive
To not love is not to live.

Pedro Basto

YOU'LL NEVER UNDERSTAND

John Mayer told me to stop your train
I wept, what a tragic-comic station.

You left and,

Dreamt of its beautiful ambiguity.

My drunken rubber-band in your pocket
And my unanswered *yippee doodle* message
Unopened in your phone.

Your letters are under my dog's pillow
The 'aimless wandering' you wanted to do
In my lonely world.

You are a thousand text words, red guitars, engraved pens
Pseudo-cigarettness
And my pagan instruction book.

Thanks for the intimacy, the silent words
About another girl.

For everything you mean to me
And so much you don't:
The incorrigible nonsense

That is you
My
Starry-eyed dream.

Ashmi Ahluwalia

MY BITCH KARMA

Admires from the window sill,
ever ebbing through her rusted boundaries,
quietly, up rises a nasty thrill.
Her fire smoulders through my crystal blue,
she will deliver clear and true.
Tingles flare through my fiendish frame,
she only has you to blame.
She's rising, advancing up through my spine,
let me be true and to myself divine.
Showing you no justice, more than you deserve,
let me out, I can't stick this demure reserve.
I plead for my fire to show,
my ashes to crisp and my auburn to glow.
She's in behind there, rattling the bars,
ready to rip out, reveal her scars.
been there all along, indignant,
watching you pretentiously do her wrong.
Destroy her, push her around,
but no more as I hit the ground.
The time has come for me to be freed,
this is no matter to be agreed.
The time is right on this unholy night.
So to you, my dear old friend,
I give it up for you, my riotous applause,
as you have self-righteously posed the cause.
Let her tear you up, unclip the chain,
and on all your lives may she be the bane.

Claire Lennox

MONOLOGUE OF ERIK

I stood in the medium heat
where every voice was measured
How often do you work?
Are you a team player?
Maybe I am –
Maybe you are –
The clock struck nothing, as I waited in the
Waiting room,
watching a wall slowly blur.
Can you play an instrument?
Can you sing?
Does that ring represent anything?
Did you see her, he said
She was something else
She was different
Not of this shelf
Do you have wealth?
I have myself!
Oh?
Oh indeed.
Will I keep the door closed –
Open the window he said
Immaculate molecules
she's made of
Intangible whirlpool her mind is.
Her cause was cautious;
I thought she was daring
Oh she is –
Yes I believe you're right –
Do you spend the night
with thoughts like these
or are you a curious type
wiped clean of prejudice
No type of stereo your mind fits;
Why thank you –
I like to think I'm sedulous
absent of meanness and callousness –
No, you're sound
No, you're sound with the volume up high
Vibrating with resonant depth.
Vibrated I answered –
What about you – I said
what about me – he said
Do you see me in you

Or is she the reminder
of reason that you see of yourself –
You're confusing me
I'm confusing you?
Would you mind if I sang a song to Nina
Who's Nina
She is, I said
What have you been calling her
It changes every day he said
What's in a name?
Shakespeare I said
Yes he said
I like Kamala he said
reminds me of a book
A myth
her ethereal movement –
she enters unannounced
No nunnery she needs –
Hello Eric
Hello –
Hello Walter –
Hello –
Have you been waiting long?
I live to wait
and I wait to live
I wait to love
If the time's right
is the time always right?
Or is it just I'm light headed
full of esteem
raised to meet your lips
sorry that was too much
No it wasn't
I declare myself
I declare myself for you
Your scent lingers
like butterflies multiplied dancing on marshmallows
Did that sound shallow?
As halo lights teach me
My fingers play the words like piano words
that I have learnt in reverie and sleep
Will I witness you weep
While I sing a potent chorus
Or will I sit stone silent
and stare
And cohort with Walter

and never falter to impress the wrong person
Do I worsen as I witness my boastful speech?
Will you reach my wavelength,
Empathise with telepathy
or just a direct meeting of eyes
tying together with nothing said
Are you a temporary fixation
stimulating my blood and pulse
a revelation before evolution took place
that same meeting
of complex interchange
the range of reasons of seasons of sanity
Is it because of my vanity
that I think you think the same
maybe not
But maybe you stare at me
Ignoring Walter like water streaming like rivers
we sit by piers and boats
hearing waves whisper undiscovered notes
sifting into air
where composers bare their brain
and let it enclose
and enfold into it
and I will hold it in solid paper
in sculpture
made by artist to artist
It will be said that it originated in a waiting room
when two men saw a woman
that caught and captivated imagination
but I will be the innovation
Walter thought there was too much passion
He had to ration his risk of love –
While I was only getting started
building up
I stood up staring at your stare
wanting an exasperated yearn
to break the seal of the mouth
and arch the eyes for dear north
will you feel the same?
I wish or I wonder
I tenderly ask for a reminder
of your name
What is your name I will say –
What is your name?

Edward Wallace

THE JOURNEY TO AN ENDLESS END

Unphased by its magnitude, I stare down its avenue . . . consider its pinnacle.
The adventure within wondering is my catalyst.
I take the first step. The compressed force between the ground and the ball of my foot is wel-
comed . . . bienvenue.
I begin walking.
My walking develops a constant . . . a self-conscience.
Time passes me by. I pass by many places. There is always 'a time and a place,' but time, I and
places are all but strangers . . . moving by with polite twinges of acknowledgement.
I maintain my constant.
I walk
I walk some more. I walk until my feet bleed . . . and walk further still.
My compass is at a loss. My moral compass is at a find.
I have travelled so far, with no sense of direction. I will travel further, to the direction of nowhere .
. . anywhere.
There is no end . . .
For each destination is the beginning of a new journey . . .
Each destination is a break and continuation of an old journey . . .
Each destination is a chapter within my journey.
Yet this is not a story about a journey.
It's just a stroll.

Jerome Asumang

THE FOX CHOIR

The road is empty and quiet
Pets all locked up nice and tight
When the fox choir comes together
With songs to embrace the night
The vixens and cubs arrive first
And have a noisy play around
The leader comes from the shadows
And utters the first wailing sound
Unearthly melodies rent the air
Blood-curdling whoops, wails and barks.
Then with a final pee on the lawn
They disband, just leaving their marks!
The road becomes quiet once more
The foxes have withdrawn.
But now here is the bird chorus
Assembling to welcome the dawn!

Stephen Mortlock

CHARLES BUKOWSKI

It was midday and he sat
drunk in the corner.
The bar was pretentious,
one 'No Smoking' table;
the bar of a hotel that
once had been quite posh.
The other patrons sat
stiff-backed away from
the drunk tramp who
spoke out of the side
of a shattered jaw.

He was clean shaven and smoked
and wore thick specs and a
black leather jacket
with fake fur on the collar,
a black beanie and a
big alkie's nose and
thick grey curls between
the back of his collar and hat.

We were told to move to
a smoking table and we
sat next to him and he told
us how and why he was dying.
An orphan at 11
a gang member at 15
a bungled robbery aged 21
and 9 years for
murdering a security guard.
'And after that, a broken man.'

But he said he was happy and asked me
'Just two favours. Be a pal and buy me a pint, and . . . '
then to butter me up
' . . . make sure you look after her!'

I went to buy some drinks and
the barman whined about
' . . . harassing customers.'
'Ah,' I shrugged. 'He's alright.'

We had to leave for
our train and as I downed
the last of Kate's beer
for her he cheered.

I read more at that point
and on the train we
christened him Charles Bukowski.

John Carter

THE CEMETERY

Absolute silence,
Tranquillity gleams,
Prayers of sadness,
Shattered dreams.

Desperation,
How to cope?
Quietly crying,
Where's the hope?

Without that life,
It's time to live,
They mean so much,
And love did give.

Scoop yourself up,
Shed a tear,
Wipe your face,
Memories dear.

Enjoy your life,
Enjoy the patter,
The love you feel,
Will always matter.

Love that person,
With all your heart,
They are still there,
At each day's start.

Josephine Bailey

THE BAGLADY'S SHADOW

Two brown carrier bags – that's all she had.
One bore the remnants of yesterday's dreams,
The other, a store of today's necessities.
I thought it sad, and watched a while.
She turned and caught my eye.
Trapped! I tried to smile – to comprehend
What torturous path had led her here.
Where were those who should be near
To ease her anguished years?
She shuffled towards me,
Tattered trainers, bandage bound,
Grasped my hand in both of hers.
Instinctively I stiffened,
Then unwound and listened,
Captured by her words;
'Don't grieve for what you think you see,
This is just a shadow of the girl I used to be.
Look into my eyes and see reflected there,
A past that dulls the pain through days of care.'

Fred McIlmoyle

JOURNEY

Struggling. In a roly-poly of questions
Mind jumping back and forth, my failing forte
Striving for a breath in this whirlpool of doubt
Yet the world keeps on drowning me, drowning me
Eyes scanning for blades to cut this rope of sad
Misery with an enchanting mask. Save me.
Change has attacked my soul, now I'm just china
Crumbled into dust with every moment of
False ecstasy. Is there still scope for me to
Reverse the timepiece and erase this deceit?

Nabila Zaman

GIVERS AND TAKERS

I see them all scrambling along the beach
Knowing that their lives may soon be out of reach
Allied troops fighting for a just cause
Exhausted and afraid with no time to pause

As they run so many picked off by mines and sniper fire
A torso here, a limb there, the carnage is dire
Just trying to stay alive in this hell on Earth
Those still running praying for all they are worth

Each and every one is a father and mother's son
Those lying dead and dying, their time is done
No one to comfort them in their last seconds
They are so noble whilst death beckons

Compare them to the profligate in Government and in the city
Who have taken what they desire without pity
Bringing us to the brink of despair
Whilst the valiant are gone, which just isn't fair

How can we ever thank these brave boys?
They got off to war without any noise
No choice but to be slain or to slay
These heroes are sent into the fray

They will make the ultimate sacrifice
At the throw of a metaphorical dice
Those that send them just take
Without concern, they are on the make

Nothing changes for those who serve their land
Splendid young men still lie dying in the sand
Destined to perish in their prime
I pray they will be remembered for all time.

Jan Smith

SHUT UP, MR SMITH!

You with the hat, and the dog, and the flat;
That squat, dull grey box of a flat. You with
Your well-tended gardens, front and back,
You paid for it, did you? Well, fancy that!
You seem a bit riled, a little upset.
It means that much to you? Now, now. Don't fret.
Odious man! It's just repossession.
Get off my back and shut up, Mr Smith!

'Don't be that guy.' – Listen to your wife.
Of course we eavesdrop at windows! We care
For your life – insignificant and small.
No one will listen. No one at all. We
Are wise and know best for you – the voices
Of society do nothing without
Due democratic propriety. Don't
Argue or question. Shut up, Mr Smith!

You know Ms Doreen, at number fifteen?
She once was your neighbour but we drove a
Wedge in-between, a JCB, so now
She is just 'her down the street'. You see, we
Flattened her house and built a new one there.
Perfect, she told us, but for the view. For
Your home's so ugly it devalues hers.
It's for her we say: 'Shut up, Mr Smith!'

A corp'rate machine? Stop making a scene!
Did you not hear what we did for Doreen?
Individual needs are top of our list
So 'tis best to be quiet. You get the gist.
What really makes me titter is that you
Think you stand a chance in this legal dance.
We've a team of lawyers and you're alone,
So give it up and shut up, Mr Smith!

Anna Hands

INVISIBLE

She sits alone at the side of the road
As the cars go by
Begging for help of a passer-by
But no one even bats an eye!

The road is dirty and hot to touch
Sitting alone, burning her bare skin
She hasn't an idea where to begin

Begging, begging for this pain to die
Passers-by, more passers-by
Yet they have problems of their own
Why help her when they can't help their own?

There was a time you know, when this lady had a home
A bed with a soft cover
Which she gladly shared with another

But the days when she had a lover were long gone
It had all started with that single bomb
Shaking the walls, crushing the rooms
And making half the people gone

They had said, 'Forever together'
When they were younger
Yet now, the deepest feeling she possesses is hunger

When she was younger she had thought she was invincible
Yet now it appears she is just invisible.

Gemma Louise Williams

THE STOBART LORRY DRIVER

From Scotland to Yorkshire, Wales and to Kent,
All over this country goods being sent,
The haulier's work is never complete,
One journey over and he's back in the seat.

Passing green fields it drives out of my sight,
Continues its journey well into the night.
The next day at dawn the weather is fine,
Up to the warehouse and made it on time.

He speaks to the staff who take off the load,
Puts on more boxes and heads for the road.
Crossroads and junctions to where there are mills,
Crosses the border and heads for the hills.

From north to south and the east to the west,
His truck is his pride, he thinks it's the best.
The driver now tired he stops for a nap,
But when he awakes he picks up his map.

Driving through villages of stone and thatch,
Along to the sea port to load on the catch.
Frozen food, whisky, goods for B and Q
Bringing everyday items for me and you.

The road haulier pulls the trailer with truck
In the wet weather it sprays up the muck,
When I'm driving behind, my wipers on fast
I wish if only I could just get passed.

It slow up the hills and speeds up going down,
Leaving the countryside, heading for town.
He sees a lorry from among its own fleet,
Travelling along it turns into a street.

A flash of the lights he waves to a friend
In other directions they pass on a bend.
Junctions with lights and a bridge over a stream
In queues of traffic a road haulier's dream!

Continual traffic, continual flow,
In all directions and onwards they go,
Where are they going to and where are they from?
Some journeys short and some of them long.

Lorries coloured red, green, yellow and brown,
I recognise the ones from my county's home town.
Armstrongs of Longtown, Stobart from Carlisle,
They're hauling the goods for mile after mile.

Some of them head for the docks with their load.
Over sea by ferry then continue by road.
Foreign number plates with letters Z and I,
But the ones I love best are PX and PY.

From farms to markets with goods for the shop,
Rarely a day do these trucks ever stop.
It finally pulls up at the company gate,
Told off by the boss as he's ten minutes late!

Helen R Hogg

HOLIDAY

Hanging on to the
fringes of the firth,
like bead ornaments,
are two severed crab claws,
completely hollowed.
I put them in my pocket.
A crow walks beside me
muttering to himself
about predestination.

Sleepy,
November light
is drooling on the
hills' double chins.
There's no one else about
and the beach has been
brushed clean as a black suit.
My feet sink
until I can touch
the skull tops.

Garry Vass

LE PETIT MORT . . .

Trapped in his arms.

I try not to think,
not to speak,
not to lie . . .

Feathered fingers trace,
drowning , , ,

breathless.

I can no longer speak,
no longer think,
no longer lie.

Cry out
and bite
and struggle
and pull him close.

Lost in another,
darkness lurks,
in shadows and I,
begin to lose the fight,

and then . . .
and then . . .
and then . . .

and then at last I give in,
and at last I am lost.

That little death,
that holds me by the throat.

Until the skin goes cold,
and the light has left,
and the dawn fades,

and he is gone.

Donna Cameron

I REMEMBER

I remember when we were young and we'd lie in bed the whole day through,
Gazing into each other's eyes, I'd curl up in your arms.
Just me and you, till out popped the moon.
We were the only people in the world.

I remember when we'd stay up on the sofa, late into the night,
Blanket wrapped around us tight,
We'd watch scary films, then could not fall to sleep out of our fright.
It was not all that bad, we held each other's hands so we felt safe.

Do you remember when the kids were very small?
We'd hear them start to wake so early in the morn,
and we would bicker, about who should get out of bed and go,
Then turns we'd take and wander to and fro.
To soothe our kin.

Remember once you had to work away. For forty nights,
I tried so many ways to get to the land of nod.
But I felt so small (insignificant) without you in our king-sized bed.
So I stayed up all night and watched our wedding video instead.
I missed your soft warm breath upon my back.

There was that time years later when I fell ill and could not sleep.
You stayed by my side and nursed me all night through.
When morning came you slumbered by my side and
I am sure I felt our once young love renew!
*In your sleep you whispered out my name
and I wondered then if you had
felt it too?*

We woke and slept together most our life,
Your soul purpose to be my husband, mine your wife.
Now as we lie here in our bed I start to weep, because I cannot wake you from your sleep.

Sharon Challinor

THE ANGEL FROM THE DEMONS

The made me with a potion using:

Seeds from the reddest apple,
This grew my talent for temptation,
A blackened crucifix, snatched from a chapel
Bound my purity my 'good' potential
A vile of lilac vampire venom
Gave me blood-red fuller lips
A nail from a witch's finger
Gave me startling predatory grips
No victim had a chance with me
Until 'He' set the real me free.

You see, demons from Hell are not the smartest,
Yes the strongest and sometimes the fastest,
But near the cauldron from which I was born;
They had imprisoned an angel whose lovely wings had been torn.
Whilst they had been creating me with dark, evil witchcraft,
Jessamine waited till their backs were turned
And pulled from above her helpless head,
Her halo burning white and gold.
With a flick of her battered wrist it sped,
Into the cauldron, bubbling blood-red.

The demons, thinking their work was done
Had left the cauldron where it stood.
But later the liquid turned sky-blue
And shimmered like a heavenly brew.

Without her halo, Jessamine fell;
Her weakened legs betrayed her well.
Her wings twitching feebly,
Spread out as she lay, leaving me.
The liquid turned a deep indigo
And as she left, I began to grow.

And every day since then I've lived a demon;
Unaware of who I was, just doing as I'm told.
I hate myself for this, but I didn't know it then;
I captured men, and knocked them out,
And brought them to my den.
I sunk my teeth into their necks,
And swapped my venom for their blood,
I hit them and I teased them, though it never felt so good.
And even though it caused me pain, I did the best I could,
To torture them, to make them feel like death by spears would.

One day like any other day I crept into the wood,
And not so very far away a knight in armour stood.
I shot behind a wide oak tree so that he wouldn't see me,
And silently, stealthily, I followed him with glee.

I waited 'til the time was right
Making sure I was out of sight . . .
I pounced when his silvery back was turned,
I seized his neck between my teeth,
And making sure it burned.
I dragged him back, after a final clout,
When I was sure that he was out.

His limp shiny body on my den's floor,
I pulled off his helmet with teeth and claw.
But what I saw made me fall
With something I'd never felt before.
The pure gold hair, the pale white face,
Made me forget the time and place.
I felt like I was lost in space.

As I leaned over him, I realised this:
I'd fallen in love, a deep abyss.
And slowly, softly, his eyelids flickered
Until he was looking up at me.

And ever since then my death-black hair,
Has hung in threads of gold;
And we live together by the sea
And will until we're old.
All my past has been forgiven
And all my evil, good riddance!
For nothing is better than our true love,
At keeping my dark side hidden.
And the bright, white halo of Jessamine
Keeps my once filthy, foul self clean.

So the soul of you
And the soul of me
Don't stand that far apart;
We both have good,
We both had bad,
And a beating heart.

Sophie Louise Rowson

A BROKEN HOME

I searched in happiness and received a list of mess
Including a picture of a happy family
The perfect one, apparently
But knowing reality a row started eventually

Maybe they missed out somebody for the picture
Maybe it was the mother being caught seeing another mister
The very same man who actually took that picture
But it doesn't matter because that moment was a perfect capture
Which helped create the sensational rapture

That they feel today and hopefully again in the future
When they look back upon this beautiful feature
They will have the same emotion as a biblical preacher
Full of hope and fantasising, love is there and never dying
Love isn't a myth, it is here and satisfying
Inside this family that never stops trying

Their hands consistently intertwining
Just to brush each other away through lying
Their hands left rough and unstable
This broken home is unable
To retract this fable
Again they turn back to the Bible
Trying to forgive the lying, deceitful and the unfaithful
So this family can reduce and finally live more peaceful.

Sheldon Sinnamon

WINTER

Oh I do adore the winter
With its frost-encrusted trees,
Its snow-white frozen bushes
The country in a freeze.

The river cast in mist
As I walk along its bank,
Slowly rising from the river
In total beauty does it rank.

I stand and look around me
At the quiet enfolding scene,
The jogger and the stroller
Leaving footprints where they've been.

I marvel at the beauty
That Mother Nature does supply,
And wonder how she manages
In these extremes, not to die.

After all, she loves her beauty
As she explodes out in the spring,
In softness and in colour
Cause the birds to hop and sing

Yet in the coming winter
As the leaves and flowers die,
She is merely sleeping, and at rest
She gently lies.

Ken Thomas

THE WILD FIRE DRAGON

The wild fire dragon lives in me,
Sometimes it cries out you see.
All conditions of her materiality,
Have nothing to do with my reality!

Like drops of dew or flashes of lightning,
Not so gentle or quite so frightening,
Agni from the sacrificial fire knows me well,
I'm part of a picture that doesn't include Hell!

The wild fire dragon lives in me,
A salamander no one can see.
I know not when she may awake,
It's usually at dawn before the day break.

Up she flares with flames red hot,
Burning with passion, the whole lot,
Then precisely at the speed of light,
Her glowing image she manifests bright.

She cannot be tamed,
She won't be shamed,
She's gloriously invisible,
Rising from a gold encrusted crucible.

Described as a mythical, ethereal material,
From which comes the creative spiritual,
Deep down from the wellspring of desire,
A flashing phoenix of inspirational fire.

She gives me all the energy that I need,
For my battle of words to succeed,
From my years at ancient Heliopolis,
To today in Brighton metropolis!

Rebirth and Ascension many a time,
Reincarnation is not a crime.
I'm the cause of my demise,
Well then that's no surprise!

You see the seed of my beginnings
Was left over from all the trimmings!
When the dragon rears its immortal head
I'm immediately interested.

When the journey is about to start,
I tune my head into my heart,
Establish a pose that's just right,
As I receive the prophetic insight.

In me the wild fire dragon lives,
In and out my breath it breathes,
It flies at speed to black wormholes,
Giving life to earthbound souls.

Doesn't matter if it's night or day,
Whether I'm at work or play,
That wild fire dragon lives in me,
Ready to spring forth immediately.

Whenever my senses are offended,
My wild fire dragon senses it.
All of it's powers increase tenfold,
And then in the vapour the dragon I behold.

Upon their faces I see the fear,
Not sure what's happening here.
Then they feel the heat come forth,
Flames of fire, the dragon's wrath!

Sometimes I think she is asleep,
When my anger I'm able to keep,
But then before you can shout fires,
My hissing wildfire dragon retires.

But on return she holds me to account,
Asking always for the full amount.
Then on admission of the dead,
Wild fire dragon plants a seed.

How much do you want to impress?
Will it that problem address?
In the crackling of the fire,
Did you locate a hidden desire?

Or did the hissing of the flame,
Simply uncover a hidden shame?
Then my dragon builds up the heat,
To ensure I suffer no defeat.

And now with wildfire sizzling,
My energy levels are bristling.
To cast forth its creative powers
Oh how the wild fire dragon towers.

And when finally her huge eye discerns,
Hanging there like a heavenly lantern,
I am brave enough to hold her gaze,
And sink into that glorious divine daze.

I marvel at the colour of her scales,
Crimson and orange with gold-tipped tails,
Her eyes a magnificent emerald green,
Truly the most dazzling I've ever seen.

As salamander powers are building,
Divine energies are lingering.
I want to make the most of this,
And feel the wild fire dragon bliss.

Since everything on Earth is free,
So the wild fire dragon tells me,
Now I want to travel eternally,
And visit all life supernaturally.

So out of homage I take off my shoes,
Believe an invisible fire element rules,
Without which material flame cannot exist,
Nor match be struck or light persist.

When the wild fire dragon starts hissing,
Think of all the things you are missing.
Earthlings only believe in what they see,
And it makes you a prisoner to your mortality.

Where is the light if not in darkness?
Looking in the mirror is egotistical madness!
Venture into the unknown and test your sanity,
In the deep space of self your flame burns brightly.

So yes the wild fire dragon lives in me,
It is a salamander no one can see.
And when finally the head and tail meet
I know I'll experience that death defying treat!

Lucy Caxton Brown

HOPE

'Hello,' said the shadow to the girl by his side
Who cried hot tears of shame, no pride
In self, no aspirations beyond the now,
The pain of never knowing the who or the how.

'I'm Hope,' said the shadow to the girl by his side,
'I'm here to show you how to turn the tide
Of forgotten strength and belief in same,
To help you see your purpose, your aim,
Your given gift of life, of love and to tame
The nagging doubts inside you head
Which undermine instead.
Like I said,
Your given gift of life and love.'

'I'm Hope,' said the shadow to the girl by his side
Who, though she still cried, had started to hear
And not to fear the outstretched hand of Hope
Which she suddenly grasped, as a rope,
To haul her out of this bottomless well
Where alone she fought her living hell.

'I'm Hope,' said the shadow to the girl by his side
Who listened intently to his mindful guide,
And watched his face light up, as if
By some magic, he could halt this suicide.

'I'm Hope, said the shadow to the girl by his side
'I have to go now, the day has died
But I'll carry on inside your fragile frame
And I will not let you go.
Remember my name.'

'I'm, Hope.'

Fiona Harris

THE BLOW HOLE

Rugged blue slate rocks line the edge of the land, ankles twist, grasping hands slip scrambling up high
To look where the sea meets the sky, I wait for the water song to blast.
For down in the hollow beneath my weathered blue slated seat, captured in time for over a century past although smaller in size maybe then perhaps.
Now shaped larger by the tide's invisible hands, the blow hole quietly stands.
Encased either side by gigantic boulders or rock, irregular mantels jut out, stepping up to the top, enticing to roam, they look darker below yet unsafe, from the thrashing of waves high, randomly thrown with abandon continuity against the cliff face.
As the tide mysteriously curls its way around to the small harboured shore, the blow hole magically comes to life once more.
Raging the sea out like a gigantic hose spraying the blue slate with white foam singing its rasping pan pipe note, wphoooooowho, wphoooooowho.

Here I sat and watched for a while as seagulls played, swooping down towards the blow hole then curving back up across the open sky it had sprayed.
I envied those seagulls, watching them brought a smile, on wishing I could fly like them into the openness, dancing wild out onto the sea, lined with its hidden caves and caverns steeped heavy in mystery.
But the sea rages like a menace when it its angry mood, dark and alluring, raising waves arching them over walls and pathways, as though trying to grab the ankles of who dares pass by.
At their own peril they go for you would only hear the seagulls cry.
Seas endured by young fishermen of long long ago who in earnest braved time after time, while bearing old hands row.
For behind small timbered doors wives with tired smiles they know wait to greet, with children, empty plates wanting food to eat.
But when fires lie cold and all lay still, babies cradled were soothed and kept gently in sleep throughout the night.
By the sea when its soul once again came alive raging out through the blow hole playing its rasping pan pipe, wphoooooowho, wphoooooowho.

If I were a being not know to Man and looked down from the sky at the view, I would notice a crevice once a whole green floor that now has been sliced in two.
On the edge of the land where the rivers run and the rain falls down into off both cliff sides, together they flow like a drain out to the ocean to be taken in hand by the tides.
While raging white waves lift themselves from the crevice, throwing up, out into the skies.
A timed pattern as though something lay sleeping, filling the air with its cries,
wphoooooowho, wphoooooowho.

Elizabeth Smith

GREAT BRITISH PEOPLE

So much love London 2012!
The athletes love their sports
The crowds love the athletes
The media love the crowds
The event loves the media
It works – we all love each other

Money has been passed to be there
Precious medals are given to us all
Respecting people for varied abilities
Achieved through hard work and love

Passion has been exuded
Tears and laughter shared
Encouragement and cheers of delight given freely
Joy and faith have been achieved within one nation
This all feels like love to me

Let's not lose these human feelings
Love they neighbour, don't lose it folks
Work hard people of Great Britain – unite
We have felt how love can be – so much love!

Paula Perkins

LIVING, BREATHING MUSIC

Music for laughter in rhythm and time
dancing, jumping and beating.
I hear it, I see it, I feel it!
Music for sadness in treble and bass
memories, sorrowful and daunting.
You taste it, you grasp it, it's real!
Music for dancing in movement and speed
loving, laughing and jiving.
Music for all in step and in pulse
serene, sublime and hypnotic.
We see it, we try it, it's ours!
Music lives on in all that we do
knowing, telling and believing.
The world's a musician, it's yours,
living, beating, and breathing,
gazing, seeing and knowing!

Sarah Wade

A BEAUTIFUL SIGH

It was dark when the day began
A million stars had died and shone upon the world
And now nothing shone
The sun was hidden behind a thick, impenetrable cloud
There was no dew and the birds were no longer singing out
In fact nothing made a sound
The milkman completed his round
But he made no sound
His float, a gliding white phantom down the suburban streets
The cul-de-sacs where young lovers meet
Where families grow and people die
The middle class, the great divide

The silence suddenly ended
A torrent of televisions suddenly switching on
But still nothing shone
There was still no sign, no flicker from the ever present sun
And if the birds don't sing, then has the day even begun?
No birds, not a single one
Children wake, a day full of fun
But no birds, not a single one
There was no blackbird, no skylark, no robin and no wren
The songs that pierce the hearts of us men
Did they die like the stars with one last cry?
An angelic encore
A beautiful sigh

Charlie Hemphrey

WHAT WE HAD THEN

When I look back, now you are gone
From this life's brief and cobbled path,
I think of all the things we've done,
The glowing ember sparkling in the fireside hearth.

Your love flies in on silver wings,
Reminding me of childhood days
When we first met, the joy it brings,
Your glancing smile, that look, your funny ways,

My love for you will never die,
The heart still beats with passion pound
Thru' all the Earth and endless sky,
Just knowing how you turned my life around.

Believe, sweetheart, in what I say,
As life goes on to pastures new,
If time stands still, come what may,
The sun will shine to warm the morning dew.

What we had then, we still have now,
In mem'ry's Book of Treasured Dreams,
We'll meet again, somewhere, somehow,
By waters clear from tumbling mountain streams.

I think of you, your presence here,
I feel your touch, so soft, so dear,
We'll meet again, somewhere, somehow,
What we had then, I know we still have now.

Tony E Warner

POETIC NUMEROLOGY

She met a stranger that day
Who had been to the depths of her heart.
Nineteenth for a clue,
And a start.
And apart from the third star
That forbade their exchange,
She decided to proceed,
And the two minds agreed to swap his astrology
For her anthology.
She contemplated his mind's melody
As he knocked gently on the door of her own.
Alikeness with destiny,
It was a peaceful interruption.
So . . .
She allowed his entry.

Their lips held conversations
Of previous deprivations
Current aspirations
Controversies
And the twenty-seven constellations.

Broken free from the moment,
He awoke memories of her role
And her rhythm
And the colours
That once filled her
Monochrome soul.
Composed of the oranges,
And the purples
And the blues
Colours she refused to now define her form.
But
Harmonic colours that would still fall each dusk.
And secretly
Rise
Each
Dawn.

As he spoke
He evoked electric emotions
And struck chords
That amplified her voice.
His tenor would trigger
Vibrations that would resonate
With rigorous vigour within her.

As the duet drew to a close
No names were exposed
And he did not disclose that
That Nine was the key
It was her path,
And it would have to be her to choose it,
On Nine's way home
She remarked the falling skies and familiar eyes
And smiled.
Silence.

She only knew then why Twelve made music.

Chereny Brown

AN APOLOGY

Five madnesses are too much for me
And I still let the wrong ones win
Free to infect as they please
Too dumb to see you keep the dark at bay
Too numb to feel the love that we both shared

As you strangle me in my dreams
My heart burns with guilt and regret
With self-loathing and shame
Too dumb to see you keep the dark at bay
Too numb to feel the love that we both shared

So all that's left to say is that
I'm sorry you weren't welcomed in
I'm sorry for everything
So sorry for everything

Roy Canty

BLUE COAT BOY

He's sick to the teeth of moving me on
Hoping and praying that I would be gone
Constabulary duties must be seen to be done
'Get on your feet or you're nicked me old son.'
I say, 'Wait a minute, I'd like to ask you
If you know what it's like to have nothing to do?
Queued up for the dole, rejected, a yob
No use anymore 'cause I can't get a job.'

I swallow the liquid, to stop me from thinking
'Lad, nothing will change if you don't stop this drinking.'
But it's warming my body, numbing my brain
Awash in my stomach, it eases the pain
I talk of my penthouse and sanitized life
My pension, my sports car, my beautiful wife

Then I grope for the bottle, turn maudlin and cross
This blue-coated boy, he don't give a toss
He grabs the bottle, I watch it go flying
To the depths of a bin, then I hear someone crying
A steaming hot cup is placed in my hand
The copper, embarrassed, says, 'I understand.'

Now I am alone and cursing the tea
Craving the booze that he's taken from me
A summons, a caution, what in this note?
Stuffed in my hand, how the bastard will gloat
Not a summons, it's bank notes, roll upon roll

Enough there to feed me, get me out of this hole
At least for tonight and several nights after
Strangers look up, as hysterical laughter
Bursts from my throat, unfamiliar, unbidden
As I ransack the bin where my bottle is hidden

Sheila Haskins

DARKNESS TO CONFUSION

Walking along with everything fine,
Just strolling down the street,
Talking or texting, music in my ear,
Simply tapping to the beat.

All of a sudden something changes,
As pain comes to my head,
Feeling weak and hard to breathe
I can't hear what's being said.

Suddenly falling to the ground,
My body begins to shake,
There's nothing anyone can do,
Just stay until I wake.

The shaking can be violent,
Incontinence is common too,
Lying there quite helpless,
Waiting for my ordeal to be through.

Finally the shaking stops,
As I start to come around,
Sitting all dazed and confused,
My head continues to pound.

It's horrible not remembering,
My body battered and bruised,
Simply waking up on the ground,
Feeling very confused.

Christopher Archibald Rooney

POEMOSAURUS READTHISICUS

For millions of years they ruled supreme on this planet
Appearing as though carved from living, breathing granite
From the smallest wee creature to the largest big beast
The reigned over the Earth from the West to the East
To discover more about these remarkable reptiles
Just study this poem and you will learn piles
I'm sure you are curious to hear my riveting lecture
If you're an inquisitive person and open to conjecture
I'm hoping if the data is in the form of a rhyme
It will stay with you longer and you'll remember it over time
So to begin at the beginning we'll name the types of dinosaur
Cerapoda, Thyreophora, Sauropodomorphia, and Theropoda makes four
These are the sub-orders to which all dinos belong
Some would include Pterosaurs but they are definitely wrong
The first and the second had the hips of a bird
While the hips of a lizard had the fourth and the third

The first – Cerapoda, were known by their osseous heads
Distinguished and classified by their huge bony spreads
Pachycephalosaurus and Hadrosaurus were examples of these
Possibly omnivorous but grazing mostly on trees
Triceratops Horridus was another example
His huge bony plate was more than just ample
In fact his skull was the largest to date
Its purpose was to attract a Triceratops mate.

The second – Thyreophora was similar to the last
Except that their tooth enamel was thin by contrast
Believe it or not this tiny differential
In classifying dinos is quite quintessential
Enhanced bone structure is a trait both one and two share
Though two had not just a bony head but bone everywhere
They were the armoured dinos of which there were legions
Prolific they were and dwelt in all regions
Ankylosaurus and Stegosaurus were just two of this kind
They had a huge plated body but the tiniest mind
Stegosaurus used his plates to make him look scary
To daunt would be predators and make them more wary
Ankylosaurus was a tank enveloped in bone
Even his eyelids seemed fashioned from stone
He had a huge ball of bone at the end of his tail
Weighing over ten stone this ball was not frail
It could fracture the leg of the meanest T-rex
With a weapon like this he commanded respect
The third - Sauropodomorphia had a remarkable girth

And in fact were the largest land animals on Earth
Their necks were as long as an epic romance
And their tails were as well to maintain their balance
The genus Diplodocus was one of the most massive
But despite his huge size he was really quite passive
However one even bigger was the Brachiosaurus
On which palaeontologists have discovered much for us
Over 40 feet tall he grew up towards the sky
At the end of his neck his head implausibly high
To pump blood to this height his heart was immense
And to bear his great weight his bones notably dense

The fourth and the last are my favourite by far
The Theropods were akin to a dinosaur tsar
A Theropod was a fearsome and colossal carnivore
With titanic teeth that ripped, slashed and tore
Spinosaurus Aegypticus was the greatest of these
He had a ferocious temper and was hard to appease
Bigger than T-rex with a long toothy snout
His powerful jaws packed some serious clout
He had on his back a big spiny sail
And strangely the female may have been dominant to the male
Raptors were another belonging to this group
They were extremely social and lived as a troop
Highly intelligent and unfeasibly fast
Their skill as a hunter has been rarely surpassed
They had a specialised claw and worked as a team
To ambush their prey or so it would seem
They ranged in size from two feet to twenty
Regarding genus and species there were certainly plenty
Despite modern depiction they were most likely feathered
Notwithstanding the contention that this theory has weathered

So now we have learned of the four different kinds
But what follows is not what one might opine
Ceropoda and Thyreophora with the hips of a bird
Became extinct on this Earth and ne'er reoccured
But Sauropodomorphia and Theropoda with the hips of a lizard
Evolved and adapted as though transformed by a wizard
Ironic it is that the fourth and the third
These lizard-hipped creatures evolved into birds.

Aly Coyle

GENERATION TO GENERATION

Generation to generation
Beautiful crafted lies handed down from father to son
Adolescence has no explanation
History is made in some poor boy's hands
People travel across the ocean to see the band

Generation to generation
Some boy with the blues
Tries to bring down the Government's plans
Wise men sleep in cardboard mansions
All over London town

Generation to generation
Two loves soaking in each other's souls
On top of the hill
Watching the city melt down
Without a moment of urgency
Their eyes were only made
To see each other's existence
In the 21st century where you can buy your hopes and dreams
In supermarkets

Generation to generation
Rock 'n' roll stars are born
Lustful poets die in their own ignorance
'Cause ignorance is beautiful
Generation to generation.

Danny Rogers

SUMMER AND WINTER

To forget you is what I desire
To admit that I think of someone I never knew
Is only a sign of the emptiness of my life.

Grass, hillside, setting sun
Summer is all around us
Warmth, the hum at dusk
Bonfires and parties
Out of our window the countryside.

To sit in the sun
You smoking an Embassy
Reading the Guardian
Sunbathing
Talking all night
Lying in your bed

Walking together
Three miles to a folk club
Arms around each other
Hitching home in the dark.

The flat land of Sweden
The lakes, the pines, the snow
Train in Alvesta Halt
The goodbye kiss
You standing holding your white dog
I board the train, sit frozen
Towns, lakes, forests flashing by
I will never see you again
I will never see you again.

Simon Nicholls

MY SAVIOUR, JESUS CHRIST

His human life began when an angel proclaimed His birth;
He was the loveliest Person who ever walked this earth.
He was full of compassion, gentle and meek,
Pleasure for Himself He did not seek.
He healed the sick, gave sight to the blind,
Restored the lame and those sick in mind.
Countless folk He fully cured –
But oh the death that He endured.

He willingly gave His back to be smitten,
'Tis in God's word that all this is written.
He offered His cheek so men plucked off the hair –
Oh the love that He showed them there!
A crown of thorns adorned His brow –
How many scars remain there now?
He was nailed to a cross through His hands and His feet –
It was here such love and torture did meet.
Pain for Himself willingly borne
'Midst cursings and spittings and constant scorn.
'Twas love for us He endured it all,
The pain and anguish, wormwood and gall

He is despised and rejected of men –
Although He is perfect, folk are quick to condemn.
He's a man of sorrows and acquainted with grief,
He knows our problems and can bring relief.
All we like sheep have gone astray
We have turned everyone to his own way.
He is brought as a lamb to the slaughter,
Submissively surrendered – He didn't falter.
As a sheep before her shearers is dumb
He silently endured – self pity? None.

The sufferings of Christ are beyond compare –
So why did He hang and suffer there?
He had the power to come down from the cross –
What made Him endure at such a cost?
'Twas love for you and love for me
The love that spans eternity.
We ourselves are steeped in sin
Not doing the things that are pleasing to Him.
Sin must be punished so that's why He hung –
Bearing God's wrath for everyone.
We need to repent of all our sin,
Have a change of heart and a turning to Him.

Acknowledging we're lost in sin and need,
And for His forgiveness we must plead.
My friend,
Jesus Christ gave His life to save us from the horrors of Hell;
If you come to Him repenting – you do well.

The words in italics are quoted from the Bible, which is God's word to us, and can be found in Isaiah, chapter 53.

Marion Tinkler

LOST SOUL

Who's that in the mirror,
Staring back at me?
The destitute figure of a man I see,
I used to stand so proud and tall,
Till my addiction took it all.
You promised me I'd stay the same,
No word of this,
Being an endless game
You lost me everything I owned . . .
Things I'll never get back,
That depressant, suppressant, life-changing drug,
The soul destroying 'crack'.
So stop staring mirror,
You lied to me,
With all the things you said.
That reflective figure,
I've recognized now,
As not me, but the living dead . . .
Mirror, mirror on the wall,
The guilty one,
In my downfall . . .

Richard Peel

EVOLUTION

There are three steps in life; I will try to explain each stage
You may find my belief rare but that does not make it strange
We will all experience it and no one will be saved
They are Birth, Life itself and the Grave
I'm a man of God, evolution does not play a part
The nine months in the womb is the way it was from the start
Adam shaped Eve from the rib beneath yet dispersed from the heart
An act of love can form a child but what emerges is His art
They way a woman is able to conceive a child on her own
I see as a mercy of God in which to lessen her load
A priceless reward for her steadfastness and patience
And the pain she endures in the last moments, are the greatest
Birth is a gift and I know this might sound crazy
But what amazes me is when she stares into the eyes of her baby
As she claws the unborn in that stage of unrest
All pain is diminished with her baby pinned to her breast
She desires nothing more yet deserves nothing less
She realises this child is her lifeline and will decide the beats in her chest
Is this evolution?
This baby grows into an infant, and won't dare grow distant
From its mother as its needs are supplied in an instant
She'll march round Planet Earth despite the circumference
Just to save her child from suffering a moment of discomfort
She'll stand through sleepless winter night and starve through summer days
She'll smile through persecution so her child does not suffer a graze
She'll play with her child while she secretly seals the pain
In reality her stomach shrivels like a crisp packet beneath a flame
A real mother is selfless, her child is the wound that she bleeds through
She will want to give and also feel that she needs to
Before she inhales one breath, her child must breathe two
As she quietly reads a bedtime story her child sleeps through
One morning the mother rises, realizing her child is not home
But before her stands an adult with kids of their own
She sits alone, cries but she can't help this
As she watches her child suffer for theirs as she did when hers was helpless
Yet this woman is at ease, and can't help but believe
That God held her child when it arrived and will support her child when it leaves
If you could use all the ink and paper you could
You could never express a woman's love for her child
So pay attention . . . look close at the angle I selected
I've made a minute examination from an outsider's perspective
To prove our existence has always been protected
Now I know what you're thinking
What do a mother and child have to do with the way life itself is depicted?

Well they say we evolved and that our bodies had adapted
Once on all fours we now stand on two, more physically attractive
The big bang was random, nothing played as a hindrance
Timed to a fraction of a second, wow what a coincidence
But what convinces me that evolution is fabrication
And that we never used branches as a method of migration
Is that the mother's love for her child defies the creation
No amount of knowledge unveils that emotion
It's one of life's slices that was stolen
The way in which you freeze a cascading tear, first time itself must be frozen
This bond is as firm as t is frail and yet cannot be broken
So I ask you . . . do not be a victim of Man's game
Love did not evolve and cannot possibly be man-made
Because our heart is a piece of flesh that mirrors our voices
It possess that which is hidden and affects our choices
A child's scream could shackle a demon with a free soul
Its scream is like tight, naked wind through a keyhole
That same sound soothes the mother's heart and caresses her chest
Her reality lies between that child's one breath to the next
The sentiment of love . . . is given as a blessing and sign from the man above
To His servants, as His chosen creation we are His workers
You will die despite the life that you lead and so I live for a purpose
If a creation exists then a creator has urged this
So I persists . . . why has your heart not reached a stage of contentment?
You are ignoring your creator so your heart has switched love into resentment
Accept that we are the descendants of a man and a woman
That's deep, seemingly bleak, we seek and perceive and weep the fact that our minds are exceedingly weak
Towards the existence completely unique
In depths we must read as to moisten and feed our brains so we are free in our speech
Hidden knowledge is as useless as the knowledge that you hold if you do not act upon the knowledge that you preach
This world consists of countless signs that you miss then have the cheek to ask – does God exist?
If we have just evolved then what would you call the connection between humans and plants?
If we did not breathe they would perish, without their oxygen we would die, is that a design or just a product of chance?
Let me simplify this into two sentences alone
In pure, simple English so we can all go home
You say we evolved from monkeys, I say it was Adam and Eve
If your ancestors were monkeys then why have you stopped hanging from trees.

Moeen Uddin

JUST US

Hair gently laps the soft shores of your
shoulders Like midnight waves of black velvet,
Eyes like the ocean bed,
Deep, full of memory
Holding secret desires lit,
By the radiance of your soul.

Lip softly curve,
Smiling at hidden passions
desires, Buried within,
The sweet perfume of your breath
Makes my head spin, filling me with
dreams Of holding you under the moon's
ivory light Kissing you while the stars
dance above, Feeling the Earth sway below.

I take your hand and draw you towards
me Bringing you close, our eyes meet
Our lips brush for the first time,
My hands caress your back,
My fingers tangle in your hair.

We stand there under the stars,
Kissing in the moonlight
Feeling our passions swell
Our hearts take wing.

And we soar over the stars,
Through a universe forged in the
fires Of our hearts' beliefs,
Filling with our minds with thoughts,
and euphoria visions.

Soft snow becomes our
bower While we lie entwined
Within the petals of the rose
Drinking dew from the other's
touch.

Lights in the northern sky dance
To a song never meant for human hearing
Bathing our embrace with polar splendor
Wreathing and twirling close enough to
grasp Far beyond our reach,

Just you . . .
Just me . . .
Just us . . .
Beyond the comprehension of all others We become one
Where one goes the other follows in their shadow
Forever one

Bound by fate
Writ by star light before
The first of life's undiluted beauty stepped blinking at the sun To
last far past the cold ending of time
Together as one we walk unafraid
For the world is ours to do with as we will
And the many spectrums of light our hideaway
And the endless skies ours to mould into what we wish

The meadow, the field, the sweet singing stream
All are made for our eyes alone,
No other has our gift of the other
None can see the mosaic made for us to live within
Where our white-winged souls drift together

Just you . . .
Just me . . .
Just us . . .
Forever . . .

Martin Hopwood

ON A VISIT TO AUSCHWITZ AND BIRKENAU

Quiet!

Hear the silent barracks echoing
To the sound of the gas pellets dropping.
I am here to witness the echo
So that my children
Will catch the whisper
So that their children will not forget.

Ron Wiener

NO MORE TESTS

If only I could pass my test
      A first class driver be,
Six times I've failed the tiresome thing
      Can't think what's wrong with me.
My poor instructor is worn out –
      The lessons never end;
And trying to learn the Highway Code
      Just drives me round the bend.

The lolly's fast going down the drain –
      My confidence is too,
My friends think it is one big joke
      Whatever can I do?
The endless switches, dials and knobs,
      The footwork and the gears,
I've tried so hard to master them
      It seems for years and years.

The lamp posts know me off by heart –
      There's quite a few still bent,
Some ditches I'm acquainted with
      For into them I went!
Disastrous are my three-point turns –
      They're something more like eight!
And trying to memorise each sign
      Is something that I hate.

Why should I bother anymore
      To take the dreaded test,
At least for the time being I think
      I'll give the car a rest.
I should have done this long ago
      And stick to what like,
And that's to get from A to B
      On my old faithful bike!

Briony V Lill

LEGAL HIGH

My friends say it's cool, and so do I,
So tell me what's wrong with a legal high?
I'm well addicted. I can't stop now
Tho' I've not really tried, so I wouldn't know how.
It's a habit I've got and I've done it a lot,
But then, for me, it hits the spot.
Week after week, I pay out more
And the more I do it, the more I score.
Before, I often feel the fear
And I make quite sure there's no one near.
I often delay and think ahead,
'If it all goes wrong, I could end up dead.'
Seconds tick by. My friends shout, 'Do it!'
They've all done it and have all come through it.
It's always the same when you take the leap:
You get so excited, the downer is steep.
You writhe and twist, your body contorted,
But if the trip's good you come down sorted.
So now I'll go for it. Climb high, look below.
Am I mad? Drugged? Crazy? I don't know.
I lift my arms, stretch, jump hard to the sky,
I somersault, twist and downwards fly.
I dive through the water. A three bubble rip!
A round of applause, a triumph. No slip.
That's why my friends say it's cool. So do I.
So, tell me, what's wrong with a legal high?

Janet Trewin

FOOTPRINTS

The sand between my toes
The warmth lifting my feet, the coolness grounding
The ease of my steps on the damp sand
The effort on dry land in fine grains of sand

A lone footprint rests
The others no longer be
Moulded back to the deep
Guided by the gentle sea

Now three or four I see
From those that walked ahead of me
A tiny paw . . .
Oh a few more
Not yet met the tide
Running free

That lone footprint
It no longer rests
Its journey moulded to the sea
Shaped by the rise and fall of the waves
Back to eternity

Moments linking in time
Every footstep to every footprint
Fading and moulding as one
An everlasting footprint
A footprint of moments

Ann Parkinson

THERE'S A CITY BETWEEN US

Traffic dampens your days at work,
Protagonists don't question its worth,
Professionals give you the eye,
On the motorways playing eye spy,
Scientists seek out the truth,
By pointing at the sky.

What will we do,
When the signal dies,
Over the streetlights,
While we communicate,
There's a city between us,
And a million radio waves.

Spring cleaning today's surprise,
Reading another financier's demise,
A daughter, a kiss and tell,
Dropping sterling into a wishing well,
Washing the ink off your hands,
For the cleanliness a visitor demands.

The satellites ring out,
In open space,
Above the blue skies
But mostly the grey,
While the signal dies
The windscreen fills with rain.

Craig Turner

SIGN IN THE STAFF ROOM AT WORK

Stay positive they said,
Stay positive I read,
Stay positive in the work you despise,
Turn a blind eye as your life goes by,
Leave your thoughts at the door,
Don't think they implore,
Pretend there is no sun,
Look out of the window at your life on hiatus for eight hours,
Can't get rid of the smell of this jail even after a thousand showers,
Take solace it's for the money that I didn't even want to use,
The books you could be reading now will only get you confused,
The songs you could be listening to now won't speak to you anyway,
Silence your mental juke box and toil for your pay.
Stay positive today,
The cash they flash, I can see on my face a fiscal rash

They say put down your pens,
Strip your pencils of lead,
Tell creativity to slumber,
Put your canvas to bed,
But can't stop us drawing in our heads,
Stay positive,
Like don't start on that waitress and treat her with chagrin,
Cos she doesn't bound over with your pie and chips with a leap and a grin,
'We've paid for this food, she better start smiling,
Or the tip it I none and the polite police I'm dialing
Have a world with yourself, she's working,
And more than that she could be hurting,
Cos John in the kitchen isn't flirting,
Or she could be wearing that frown,
Cos she's realised she's only got £30.00 for her night out in town,
That's not much when you consider the taxi back,
Plus after she's done serving you she's got dishes to attack,
But no, she has a grimace,
She's finished.
We have all felt like her, bit lonely and that,
Stay positive.
Stay positive,
Cos sometimes words cling to the air,
Like candyfloss to hair,
And birds sing for their bread while the cat bosses stare
At the endless charade of hierarchy,
John then Paul than George then Starky,
But star key unlocks the door to the skies,

Hope is life, I summarise,
There's beauty in your summer eyes,
Don't count the calories in pies
Dietary information often lies,
Distracting from the truth with garish rides,
That only seek to compromise,
Our promise and delightful ties,
Forged from friendship not to buy,
Feel your waist and touch your thigh,
Dietary information often lie
Love is all,
No chance to take,
No dast to cie,
Be brilliant and hear them sigh,
Stay positive.
I feel like,
Tintin going exploring,
Paths opening up, new days dawning,
I'm done with yawning, it's a waste of breath,
I don't feel lethargic, I don't feel bereft,
Heads down, give me a test,
About anything cos this beat in my chest,
Means I'll beat Kasporov at chess,
Armani couldn't make a sexier dress,
Alleviate stress quicker than Prozac,
Cut the beanstalk down faster than Jack,
I can stretch my mind more than the guy on the rack,
Cos if our lips locked together we could throw away the lucky heather,
No more boring day of monotony,
Fingers crossed, watching the National Lottery,
Not just waiting around thinking *I'll chill,*
But striving for the horizon over the hill,
Stay positive.
But the best thing I saw recently,
Was when I'd just finished my tea,
And I saw these two old folk, who live near me,
One about 89, the other 93,
Twilight of their lives to say the least,
Real hunched and stopped over, all false teeth,
But the way they held each other's hands the tenderness was palpable,
Cradled and soft, the care undoubtable,
Cos some things are not withered by age,
They stick thorough life to every page,
Decrepit vocal chords that would have a job to sing,
But their demeanour hits the high notes, bellowing love's the greatest thing,
And whatever they think the next life is Earth, air or above,

At least the opening gambit can be, 'We ended that one with love'
And everybody wants that, everybody,
Everybody with this life to live,
Peace be with you and bless you
And stay positive!

Simon Soane

THIN SEAM

That day,
that summer –
we lay beneath
a sheer cliff
mighty above us.
you talked to me
about millennia
and climatic change.
aconites, strata,
rock types, thin seams
and their significance.

Your head was framed against the cliff,
I felt the warmth from your body,
saw your eyes reflected the light
on the sea,
and how in the breeze your hair
danced like straw.

Dawne Clively

THE CHARITY SHOP . . .
(GILBERT AND SULLIVAN STYLE)

An elderly couple , Dorothy and Pat, were shopping in the high street – looking for a hat,
'Let's visit that charity shop and see what they've got.'

Chorus of customers – bystanders – to one another,
They've come in here to buy a hat! Can you believe it? – Well fancy that!

And they were faced with such a display – they were quite amazed – and so little to pay!
Elegant hats from a bygone year – men's hats, ladies' hats – even hats made of fur,
'Which hat do you like dear? – At these prices we could afford *two*.'
'Oh no dear husband – *one* will do.'
'There's a nice hat dear, over there by the chair.'
'That would do nicely, dear husband – suitable for both of us to wear.'

Chorus of customers . . .
Only one hat for both of them to wear? We can't see how they could manage that –
They'd need to buy at least a pair!

Wife turns to customers for advice:
Well, who do you think should wear that hat? Should it be me – or should it be Pat?

Long pause as customers confer amongst themselves.
We don't know dear – but to be honest and true –
We suppose it would be suitable – for either of you.

Wife – in loud tones of jubilation –
So you think that hat is suitable for either of us to wear?
Just image that – A bi-sexual hat!

Customers begin to mutter in disgust –
A bi-sexual hat! Whoever heard . . . A bi-sexual hat! Don't use that word . . .
A bi-sexual hat! It can't be true . . . A bi sexual hat! Can I have one – too?

Audrey Evans

JUST ANOTHER BIRTHDAY

The years are flying fast it seems
Why only yesterday, I was in my teens
Now I find my sense of humour waning
And it seems I am always complaining
All my bones creak and groan
It's getting hard to hear on the phone
Glasses I wear, for my failing sight,
And my teeth, I can take them out at night.
My waistline, yes that's certainly spread
And my sex life, well that's stone dead
I seem to get a new wrinkle every day
But I suppose that's the price I have to pay
I've lived my life, oh so bold
And now I guess I am just 'bloody old'
But I wouldn't change a day you see
''Cause this is my life, this is me
So when I am dead and laid to rest
Please, please remember me at my best.

Faye Giffard

AGAIN

Maybe if I take one step back,
I'll slide forward two.
Maybe if I stray off this road
I'll still make it home.

Maybe if I close my eyes tight
I'll see the true path.
Maybe if I starve my fat mouth
I'll have room to grow.

Maybe if I put away my guns
I'll still win the war.
Maybe if I try to believe
I will need no faith.

Maybe if I climb down the hill,
I'll improve my view.
And maybe if I listen less hard
I'll hear the birds sing again.

Phil Binding

LOVE 318

I'll cut off your face
And wear it once in a while
Looking in the mirror
I can again make you smile.

I'll cut out your voice box
And sew it into my throat
So I can hear your laughter
When we hear a joke.

Shaving off your hair
I'll put it in a bag
Run my fingers through it
When I'm feeling sad.

I hope you understand that what I'm trying to say
Is I need you with me every minute
Every hour
Every day.

Paul Brookes

DAISIES

Daisies
Day's eyes
Bright yellow
White 'lashes'
Blink open
In sunshine
See hundreds
Look thousands
Something small
Something special
Yellow middle
White petals
Green grass
Blue sky
Beautiful
Flowers
Daisies.

Stephanie Hale

NO MORE THE ACTOR

Worked with and touched the lives of those from theatre past, not now
Proud achievements, with those whom I shared the stage, I bow
Faces flash by, performers left behind, appear before me
Now retired, memories of past drama experiences stay, with clarity I see
Costumes no longer needed hanging, stored gathered for theatre, crowded
Waiting in line, bunched up together gather dust, and grounded.

A character made good by dressing up, made up, is no longer
No more the actor performing, entertaining, over time had grown fonder
Costumes changing, switch into, colourful or not the character it reaches
Bold and bright, dark or shabby, inspiring the step into role it teaches
One play required, stage right, each night seven costume changes
Success achieved with Velcro-stitched, helpful hands, in turning pages

Inspiring it can be to build a different character, to develop a unique role
Able to grasp the person, reach the part, reach the nature, the soul
Make-up applied with skill can sharpen, emphasise the humorous or feared
Can introduce a new face with moustache and or hairy stick-on-beard
Others advise, 'You'll look pale, washed out,' need to paint face in layers,
Wash off, after show, ensure head in sink first, in front of other players

Before rehearsal, working at the word, when spoken as if it is part of me
With emphasis and ownership remaining the purpose, the key
Holding up to the gathered crowd, so it feels true and gifted
Dialogue that's made audible, the voice thrown, the audience lifted
The pace a consideration, that it moves, excites in the hearing
Performance is quick, lively, silences more telling, powerful and stirring

Having read and learned the chosen script, a readiness to perform
Engaging audience in storytelling, energy to take the theatre by storm
But when, 'no more the actor' comes also a sense of loss, a thinking shift
A time realised, the outcome is only as good as the last selling pitch
Better the period when engrossed in the acting craft, attractive a desire
That time so involved, you think it an interest, of which you'll never tire.

Ronald Constant

SLEEPING ANGEL
(In loving memory of Shyla Reanne Grenney 1992-2011)

A heart of gold
Memories of you will never grow old
You gave us all reason to believe
Now sadly it is time for you to leave

This world will not be the same without you
Every day was a battle
But you showed nothing but courage all the way through

Every moment spent with you will be forever cherished
Your memory will carry on and shall never be perished

Life is so hard without you around
But at least I know you are smiling down

I am happy to know you can finally rest now
The pain you endured is no more
For this loss of you I wish there was a cure

Now you are with the angels it is time for us to part
You will never truly be gone as you will always be in our hearts

As you are looking down from above we want you to know you filled our hearts with love
Goodbye dear friend
Goodnight, God bless
Our sleeping angel.

Chris Tucker

TRIBUTE TO A WORKMAN

I used to work with old Jack,
And, with a bound bag on his back
Time and touch had ploughed his face
The flux of the years had soldered him
As hard as brass.
His thick arms fascinated me,
And his vinegar smell hung heavy
On the gaseous air.

At times he looked
As grotesque as a gas mask
As he thumbed and flicked
The torch's wick about
And heaved the stubborn metal off;
In the hammered dark
His only oratory
Was the silver curl of the swarf.

Life was simple then,
But fathered as I was
I lost my hopes
Among those wheels of fire
And banging sparks.
But old Jack loved the fierce trade
His honest sweat had shaped and made.
Wisdom talk through him like quenched steel.

I watched him long
At what his craft had done,
His hard hands,
Shaped by the heat of the years,
Smashed the heavy punch
And stroked the boiling solder slow;
He taught me there
More than any school would know.

Those rhythmic days
Were more than mechanical to old Jack,
They were as bright as bearings,
I've seen him, bull-like,
Powering the mighty stocks,
And, bowing his oily brow,
He'd pound the blue chisel in;
Life as sweet as tea to him.

Hammering home the nails,
Old Jack was an iron man,
Mighty among his stuff;
But one day, bag-bent on his business,
Intent as a tin-smith,
Death took him, shock-sudden,
His wrought pipe bent and rough,
And his bag bound like a sheaf.

Michael Hurn

TODAY

This din is killing me
I don't want to hear all of this noise
It's getting louder and louder
I just want some peace
Some inner relief
Some saviour of sorts
The world is against me: cohorts

Aggressive, demanding people day by day
Not a thought about how I feel . . .
Or an ear to what I could say
This society is fractured: disarray

Everybody is in such a rush, the trains are crushed
The shops are brimming, is it a recession, or am I just not winning?
On the opposite side frustrations arise
Brought up in a wasteland, so much to despise
No bright sunny day; just poverty and greed
At headlocks now – just who will succeed?
Governments are headstrong
Poor people considered wrong: *big problem!*

Brimful of Asha on the other side
It's jackanory – I reside . . .
Someone needs to tell this story (I for one am not for glory)
The bittersweet of the poor: who's ready now?

Andrea Earwicker

WHO'S TO BLAME

Remember when you're angry as a nuclear rocket
With enough power like a static socket
Seeing a man reach into your pocket
Stealing a valuable gold locket
You want that thieving scum to stop it
But who's to blame?

Is it the fault of his young childhood that didn't do him any good?
Parents neglecting the real essence and responsibility of 'parenthood'
Social groups that made him steal what he could
Though without the temptation he probably never would
But who's to blame?

Is it the society we live in that begins the tale?
The social pressure that makes individuals frail?
The immense problems that make us go off the rails?
Lack of education that makes our brains turn stale?
But who's to blame?

Is it the quality of education we give our children to learn?
To develop them as adults, to grow up and be stern
The media's influence to make their feelings churn
Separating love and hate, causing emotions to burn
But who's to blame?

Is it the media that brainwashes our minds?
To believe the unthinkable and divide boundary lines
For us to accept the unclear and unkind
Which is aimed at people who are of different kinds?
But who's to blame?

Is it the solution to hurt those with a voice to say?
To kill those who are different in every way?
To torture individuals mentally and physically each day?
To teach hate throughout generations to stay?
But who's to blame?

Is it the religion we follow to make us reform
To repent our sins and make us reborn
To cleanse the soul from spiteful scorn
To worship a God that will always live on?
But who's to blame?

Is it the genetic evolution which added to the scientific revolution?
That made this senseless conclusion
For there to be no resolution
How can we ever dismiss the logical exclusion . . .

We are to blame.

Tanya Davis

AN INVITATION TO OLIVIA STONE

Come away and love me
Come away and die with me

Touch me in a world you have never touched
Whisper the wild sounds we wash around our mouths
When our wet tongues wish for an extra vowel

Come let me kiss you in the wide open fields
Come let me kiss you will the grass sheds her green

We could split rainbows in the age of money
We could break so gently the silence cracks
My hair in your hand and your hand in my hair
With no luxury greater than that of our bodies

Come away and love me
Come away and die with me

Where the owl's wing ripples the velvet moon
Where the huge waves refuse the sad dolphins
Together, like in dream, we weave from each

Tell me goodbye will not be our last
But the first that echoes every cloud
When the north wind melts the south

Come away and love me
Come away and die with me

Charlie Baylis

ONE UNDER

i

The morning of one under
Was cold and dark
Ordinary and miserable,

The same as every morning.
I snapped at my wife,
Ignored my daughter,
Disrespected my life
My unhappy existence.

The morning flies buzzed
In my ear as I trudged
Unseeing to work.
To my underground job.

I traveled from dark to dark
To dark.
Lenny gave me a cheerful wave,
A ray of light –
I managed a nod.

Bakerloo, Bakerloo, let it be
Bakerloo –

Northern Line. A stab
In the dark.

Halfway through –
Mind the doors –
Sorry for the delay –
Sardines, no humans.

Then she came.

ii

The morning came –

The clouds had parted
And the sun shone on my soul.

No one said a word,
The peace was overwhelming –
'No more' it said.

I was naked
My skin prickled with electricity
The underground was waiting.
It expected
I obeyed.

I ran.

iii

A blur
Red lips smiling
Brake, brake
Life blown apart

iv

The morning of the funeral
The sun burned
In a pure blue sky.

I held my daughter
So very tight,
Tighter than life.
She squirmed and giggled.

My wife – blonde hair
Against black, so beautiful,
Wiped my tears away
Tenderly.

Later her father came,
Shook my hand –
No hard feelings, he said
She was disturbed, he said
Nothing I could have done, he said.

I didn't say that
Guilt had burned my soul
Clean.
I didn't say that
I was no longer
Blind.
I didn't say that
His loss had become my
Gain.

v

At her graveside
The smell of lilies
And damp Earth
The priest says that her troubled spirit
Is now free.
And mine soars
With hers.

Ruth Coleman

FRESH AND NEW

I feel the need, a growing need
to get back to this and feel this bliss,
and you will find your peace of mind.

When the water's flowing I feel I'm flowing;
by the water's side I feel I hide,
it nurtures me, the stream I see,
the peacefulness mesmerises me.

I look out to the sky as far as I can see,
and know that this is where I want to be.
Not in sadness anymore,
a tremendous feeling, I'm in awe.

The sky's so blue I feel it too,
the sunset penetrates right through.
It takes away the pain from me
and fills me with a new vitality.
My memory is fresh and new –
when I see the early morning dew.

The buttercups don't waste their time,
standing tall they're not hard to find.
The deep, deep yellow reflects the sun,
and the green, green grass is luscious too,
I embrace this and I take this as a sign of life; that is so rife.

And when I see the stars in Heaven,
I know that I am really in Heaven.
This special moment that I see
I wonder and dream at what I will be.

I'm thankful for another day,
and know that life's worth living!

Liz Everett

LEARN TO CRY

The tears I cry
Are bitter and warm
They flow with love
But take no form

I cry to myself
Coz I can't take it
Filled with an anger so immense
That I have to break it

Can you feel my pain
Through the words I speak?
Would you listen to my heart
If I decided to teach?

I imagine then I die
After I die I fly
But before I fly I cry
Then I can say goodbye

Close your eyes
And listen to me
Feel your heart drum
To the sound of the beat

And then take a look
With your eyes closed
And dream in your life
That you're opening doors

Metaphorically speaking
Touch yourself
Try to embrace it
Coz you're nobody else

And when the world is over
And we've said our goodbye
I'll sit and wait
And then learn to cry

Don't be afraid, this is just a ride
The fear of life comes from inside
Don't believe them when they say
Coz only you can take your pain away.

Daryl Evans

THE PROGNOSIS OF A PASSIONATE MAN

Though life is submissive to none
A transcendental condition of
Success is the belief that you
Can handle the tests coming your way.

Silent no longer, let me reveal –
If you give up, or practise pessimism,
You've already lost.

Life consumes the weak.

They say the 'stars align' –
But I don't believe it.
No God – no gods – no mysticism.
All we have are the hands we are dealt.

We're all gamblers – and life is never equal –
But those who win big
Always stake the most.
It's not as dramatic as it sounds.

No cliché bullshit, 'high risk/reward'.
No: I stake my whole life on a single spin
A single number – 21– and eat, breathe, drink and love
The things I do.

If you aren't passionate, you're already dead.

Luke Labern

UNTITLED

Forgive me, for the parched lips of my heart speak poorly of love
and the tremble of loneliness; treasured behind the dancing smiling lies,
strangles and chokes my voice and I drown in the silence of my thoughts' abyss.
I gaze in childish wonderment; the wild frenzy world of words,
and it voices the song my soul sings.

Chaitanya Dorwat

THE BLACKBERRY YEARS

The world was big in the blackberry years
and sun-kissed, scrumpy apples fell
we ran and played those barefoot days
and measured time by churchyard bell.

When black-faced miners trod the roads
with coal-dust voices – thick on the air
I loved you then as I do now
my own sweet love – 'My cariad mawr.'

When the world was small in the autumn days
and golden leaves did shed the trees,
we'd talk and walk the well-known path
and the blackberry days all were gone.

When the world was old and lanes turned cold
and winter's touch caressed your cheek,
you took my arm with a gentle care
and all of my life, and you were there.

Catherine Moran

UNTITLED

My children/grandchildren bring overwhelming, overflowing love in my heart
Many good things I recall when we are apart.
Milestones have passed and gone
But the memories and love go on and on.
A mother/grandmother God's gift to me
Nothing more worthy will there ever be.
My heart refills never empty of love
Returned by my family and the good Lord above.
I am aging and slowing but just one smile
From any of them makes my life worthwhile.
A phone call, a visit, a hug without doubt
A mother, grandmother can't do without.
All of these things keep my heart overflowing
With love just growing and growing
Words can't describe the joy, the uplift
Of children and family, God's gift.

Barbara Irvine

RETRIBUTION

They walk behind you old man Seth
Their eyes as black as coal
You can't escape the smell of death
It's rotting in your soul.

It's cold inside the woods tonight
No light from moonless skies
They're all around – scream as you might
No one will hear your cries.

They'll get you Seth – this lifeless pack
Go look into your fire
The blooded fleece upon your back
The entrails in the mire.

Remember Seth the screams, the pain
The terror in their eyes
The sodden ground where they were lain
No mercy when one dies.

Make no mistake, it won't be quick
It could be trap or wire
Or studded boot – a well-aimed kick
Be sure it will be dire.

You're doomed old man – go run in fear
Get on your knees and pray
Know this – it is your last night here
It's time for you to pay.

You cannot flee Seth – feel the fear
They're snatching at your breath
The once proud stag, swift hare, young deer
Now hunger for your death.

The crows will peck your eyes out Seth
The dogs will drink your blood
They all will revel in your death
So wretched in the mud.

Irene Gofton Brown

186

SKIPPY

I was ready to visit my brother-in-law
but a family emergency created a flaw
My nephew, it seems, was locked up in jail
my late sister's husband wouldn't post bail
Not a good time to visit
I'd already taken time off from work
a trip to Vegas, what could it hurt?
I packed a bag and loaded the truck
off seeking fortune with a wee-bit of luck
Oh, what fun
I checked into a room, then hit the floor
riches awaiting time for a big score
I found a crap table, it felt like we'd met
I pulled out my wad and placed a big bet
Come on, Lady Luck
I could not lose, kept letting it ride
the Dame of Fortune stayed on my side
Eventually it ended, I needed to pee
a grand for the croupier, and the rest was for me
$43,000 and change
I relieved my bladder, up-graded my room
called an escort service, cranked up the tunes
I partied all night with Trixie and Carmen
brings an old man to tears, the fun was alarming
Breakfast and off to the circus
By chance Trixie's friend was the animal trainer
she told him my story, his reply a no-brainer
'I've got a young elephant that needs a good home
thirty K delivered,' 'I want him' I moaned
Skippy was his name
He arrived real early the other day
on a great big truck loaded with hay
He came with some stuff and real big book
he likes his new home, I can tell by his look
He even likes my kitties
He goes with me on my every-other-day walks
down our country road, the neighbours gawk
Upon a padded saddle ride my cats
they purr to him, and he rumbles back
one big happy family

Brad Barrow

SAVAGE HOUSE

It was a book on decluttering that started it all,
It said our house was too big and we needed it small
So off we went to look around,
It was not long after that we found,
The house that was just right,
But we viewed it in the night.
Well 4 o'clock to be exact
But it was just getting dark.
We pulled up on the driveway as it had a place to park.

We went in and I said, 'Oh that's lovely, look a chandelier,
The curtains don't look grubby and it has a lovely atmosphere.
We'll buy it,' I said, 'as we want to downsize.'
I went home to declutter not seeing our demise.
'We don't need all this stuff, let's throw it away,
Most of it's dated, faded and grey.
We'll get some new things and make it look nice,
This house is the one, we needn't think twice.
It's a little over our price,
But what's a few weeks of beans and rice?

Moving day came and it all went well,
Until we entered, the 'house of hell!'
I thought something amiss when we noticed a smell,
I felt a sickness inside that was hard to quell
And when I saw them I nearly fell.
The previous owners, so thoughtful and nice
Had left in the cupboard two dead mice.
There were slugs in the kitchen, one in the sink
That made me aquiver when getting a drink.
The electric's not safe and the kitchen all rotten
And cleaning was something that had long been forgotten
There was woodworm in the hall
And the bath was not attached to the wall.
Then the boiler broke down and the TV wouldn't work
As the aerial was not of the right sort
And when it rained it poured down the wall
As the gutter was not where it ought.

We fixed what's not safe, but the money's run out
Should I pull out my hair, should I scream and shout
No! I've decided it's best if I sit for a while,
I have a new book in my hand, and soon I have it planned
It's all about a new look you can get with no wage
It's called 'rustic' and it's now all the rage.

Julie Boitoult

FLASH POEM #1

On closer inspection
I could see the flaws,
nothing too serious of course
a few lines gone over here and there
and some inconsistencies in the shading.

They reminded me of the time
we wandered around that gallery,
oh, where was it now?

And you said look – look
a child could do better than this
it's all squiggles and scribbles.

I don't think it's quite as easy as that
I remembered saying,
partly under my breath and surprising myself.

Cue disapproving look,
your Paddington hard stare I called it.
Never to your face though . . .

Jonna King

THE COLOUR OF VOIDS

Look around and see what I see
The birds hugging
In Human smiles,
A heart that melts
Yet has no pot
To melt into,
Emotions rumbling in tumbles
That pens and minds alone
Can grasp.
Search around and feel what I feel
Heartbeats on relay races
Loving without being loved,
The filling inwards
Having no externals to own
Expressing expressions of lack's care
When wanted and abandoned
Reach the mortal,
Translated to immortality.
I love to love,
Would you love to love?

Okeke Akudo Nkemjika Christien

MY GODDESS

When God commissioned,
You to be made,
Heaven and all its Angels,
Were given three days,
To rest, reflect and rejoice,
For what they had created,
Even God had a lump,
In his throat when he saw,
His angels' labour of love,
You set a precedence,
In Heaven 'my love'.

Rob Abdul

WORDS . . .

Without you, life is nothing.
It's a kind of sadness, I feel the pain.
A knife in my neck, I try to survive
But life is stronger than me.

Words . . .
We love talking about me and you
We love talking about stupid things
But we forgot that we need to live.

Birds flying next to you,
You try to reach them,
To touch the sky and feel it like the grass in your garden.

Learning, teaching, thinking
And still dying.

Florentina Ivan

DAMAGE

From one damaged ego to another
The blind drives a spike
Into another mind
And a whole person is fractured
The cracks spread through a family
Pieces no longer fit easily
Dislocated emotions flounder
Confused in lights and voices
Until refuge may be found
In the safety of a locked ward
And the comfortable straitjacket of drugs
Still the wound remains untreated
The spike is still lodged
Blurring the vision
Until you are forever blind
Be careful
Lest you damage another mind.

Attracta Walsh

THE FULL CIRCLE

buzzards wheel above jumbled cliffs
loud zoo of the zodiac; squawking pheasants ragged
the tide churns blossom to rotten pulp

an explosive sunrise
cancers interviewing clouds
floating like lilies motionless in the scarlet sky
thicksome bloats of bruises grow

huge motion of mothswarm, by god it roars
wild-scattered waste torn to pieces
by spectral moons rippling on troubled waters
count the stars and satyr bears the boneface
an incubus of vulture-like libido, napalm on his breath
cutting a circle into the long, long skies

cameras hide in heaven's basin
a dionysian sex ghetto, rust
animals ripe w/ gonorrhea
and vulnerable to sexual mysteries
life cycle depends on prehistoric dharma of the body

sublime motor activity, kittenish and fanciful
opens the lid of some holy void yes zoom
bruising dawn at mother's core
fragile as drops of dust
frayed sounds of circuit sparks

moody black heaven literally burst inside and out
celestial wind sucked backwards into volcanoes
tumbling floods look upon the dream in silence

under thirty fathoms of saltwater
eight rows of teeth; the torn breast of a mother
she is nursing sharks and stingrays
her moods deep like the moon's seed planted, oh the meteor gleam!

unhinged through involuntary hypnosis
cold cloisters of vision
diamond bleakness of the pristine lake
consider the nakedness of water
translated science of minimal feeling

ring of roses sucks the tears from a sniper's rifle

thin shadows of mind and spirit, hermit's mossy cell
where wild beasts find pine and roses
and man, with weary feet, finds thorns
solitude bonier than age

flowerpot clamps like an iron maiden
grow downwards, brother plants
biblical rain thrashes the warped ridge
words and dream and tragedy

Lars Donohoe

ARTIST'S MOUTH

I sing of Man –
Of that thunderous beating to live – and tell
Of life and troubled pleasure.

(A voice descended through generations:
a muse invoked;
Atlas speaks a thousand tongues.)

The tongue trips to tell a tale
Of love and midsummer scents –
The inner eye sees sweat on shirtsleeves
And mouths that seek each other through the haze;
Reel back to their own misremembered memory
Of youthful infatuation.

A daughter is laid flat to rest,
Lost to the elements;
A father gasps and grabs –
Her warm skin is pale in the stage-light.
He rises, born again in sorrow;
The audience weeps and smiles.

Words, like bullets, soar from the teller:
Trenches collapsing in a dull cascade.
Huddles of men, flickering lights piercing the darkness,
Whisper mutely into the gloom: 'Dulce et decorum est';
Distorting, mutating, constantly retold.

I sing of Man – of life and troubled pleasure.
The heart is cleansed, the mind refreshed
By worlds and mouths
And once – upon – a – time –

Matthew McConkey

DIVINITY OF LOVE

The onset of teens, brought many a dreams;
quite visible in our sparkling eyes.
We were two bodies, yet one soul;
bond by everlasting friendship tie.

One day I noticed a certain charm on her face,
with her lips adorned by a mesmerizing smile.
She told me she was in love.
And gosh! It in fact changed her style.

She used to speak a lot regarding him,
which I had to listen, with a put on grin.
And gradually the thought of sharing her,
somehow crept in-between.

She was perturbed at my behaviour;
I myself was lost you can say.
And the last thing we could do;
was finally part our way.

After a decade facing her today,
in an alien land was quite a shock.
She was the one to greet me first,
encouraging my lips to break the lock.

Though she was speaking,
I was searching for my bubbly friend.
in the figure, in front of me;
who was quite subtly blend.

I mustered up courage to ask
regarding her love, after so many years.
And in place of an answer, I could just get,
a pair of eyes filled with tears.

Thereafter what she told me, was a saga of her days gone by.
The happy moments she shared with him, were too feathered to fly.
And just before they were going to be engaged,
he left for his heavenly abode, without bidding her a goodbye.

Though being a most eligible spinster,
she couldn't think of marrying somehow.
So she dedicated herself to a cause,
and has a purpose to live now.

He had always helped orphans,
as he himself was one.
So she had started a charitable orphanage,
being the mother of all and one.

She was narrating, and I was feeling,
my heart was going to crush
She had become a figure larger than life
because of a divine feeling called 'love'.

Shweta Khanna

AYSYMMETRIC INFATUATION (PAINTED FROM A SHALLOW LAGOON)

Hearts clinging in mutual mucus;

Me the clownfish
sheltering, shielding
in blank-minded
tentacles; you
the anemone
sapping the school
harpooned by my
flamboyance;

Me the frail . . .
gleaning all algae,
isopods; foes
of your hairy
back, flapping
flimsy fins
to ease our
underwater spree;
yet you wait
impassively
till I'm devoid
of mucus,
to prick my
dryness,
prick to
death!

Raymond Uyok

AS I PASSED THROUGH THE STREETS OF ENGLAND

I walked through the streets of an unknown country
    To feel the luscious smell of that land,
It marked an everlasting spot on my memory,
    With the wonder of meeting people so grand.

I stopped at crossings to see the vibrating fast cars
    And people in jackets or coats of every hue;
I met the boy who delivered the morning papers
    And chose to tread on the narrow lane in lieu.

Those narrow lanes had winding cobbled streets
    With many narrow alleys,
Reminded me of the Pied Piper from stories of myth
    Who enchanted the valley.

Lacy curtains hung on doors and windows,
    The looks filled with an indifferent air,
I moved on through the misty fallow,
    To know England with interest and care.

Some cottages moaned in the faint light,
    That was blackened with moss,
Some other gleamed so gaudily bright,
    With gardens where flowers made a toss.

I felt the pounding heart of the city,
    As I entered in a busy market;
The shopkeepers made deals so witty
    As pounds came flowing to their pockets.

I met a father in a dark black suit
    Holding his child's hand so tight,
And also an old man without a tooth,
Waiting at the signal for the green light.

Beautiful women who dyed their hair
    Passed with cigars in their hands;
Some were mothers with shoulders bare
    To feel the sun and get them tanned.

There were men with tattooed arms,
    With long hair or bald head for show,
With warm smile they spread their charm
    From a boy to a man as they grow.

No one saw me stopping here and there
    To experience the fresh smell of mystery;
I steadily headed far and near
    And stopped by the gravel in a cemetery.

I journeyed on foot in that doleful place,
    Where destiny ordered the souls to rest,
It enthralled the air with deep silence,
    Except the chirping birds in their nests.

I passed through roads both converging and diverging
        And gathered memories strengthened with knowledge,
The ineffable happiness it did bring
        Which bird feels, once set free from its cage.

Paramita Chakraborty

India

KNEELER'S LAMENT

Words dripped out through tears
sent out and up to heavenly ears. Problems
of any magnitude
– my problems,
need more than a gentle touch.
I seek the knowledge of the omniscience. Patience
being a virtue is asked for in a gush of breath.

I have so much to ask.

Waiting
– unknowing,
if I'm heard.
Though the stars seem to glow brighter. Leaving
more questions.

Being free isn't so freeing.

Kneeling down, bent forward, I begin again. My
list longer for it is a new day. Tomorrow
who knows how long I shall whisper to Heaven?

Patricia Ferraiuolo

A GRANDMOTHER'S KALEIDOSCOPE

Pickaxes and hammers
resonate on the stones
and planks of her heart.

An ancient mansion
loses its head and shoulders,
then its torso too.

His hidden life in Malaysian woods
during an old war,
usual silence of the empty nights
near her granary,
which was always filled to the brim,
scary night wind rattling in the lone window
of her top storey,
compensating ecstasy of the reunion
here in an Indian village . . .

O Grandma,
I see your yellow kaleidoscope.

Broken stones and planks are heaped up
before the shrunken emotions.

She watches from the kind veranda
of her son-in-law.

O Grandma,
the present is only a ghost
of the past in your kaleidoscope.

Fabiyas M V

THE JOKER

The circus deserted
and shows stalled
People
grunts all around.
The evening threatening
to be darker than ever.
The joker stabbed a couple
with his knives, one on one
He must be killed, for
His eyes are so coloured.
And before he came to us
he entered the House of Mirrors
he never removed the colours and hues
His hands strained with yellow and blue.
He must be killed, for
His eyes are so coloured.
We did not wait for him
to come and plunder us all
So we took what we had with us
and barged open the door
Inside, we saw not one but many
A shades of that joker
As he slit his wrist, we saw a pale red
Colour, all the colours he bore
But the joker must be killed, for
His eyes are so coloured.

Priyanka Dey

BEFORE IT GETS TOO LATE . . .

When you go away and when you are a distance far away from me,
Or for a long time you don't speak to me,
Each moment feels like thousands of years,
That's when I lose control over my heart and mind,
And both of them start thinking what they were never supposed to.

When don't I feel that you are the same soul I loved since a long time,
It's now when I have to love up to the old memories by lying alone on a dead bed,
Craving it to bring it into life by taking your mind back,
When it was alive and I was in your arms and I felt life in your breath.

When do I feel just like moving monotonous on a road with strangers,
Heading nowhere in a lost direction with no cause or intentions,
When I look back to the time when you hugged me through my body sitting behind me,
And just then my smile would say all and feel that I need no one else,
Because I have built my own world on these two wheels itself, with you.

I wish you to talk to me just to make me remember what your voice sounds like,
And when you don't -
I feel like a sword stuck halfway pierced into my heart through my mouth,
And leaves me dead with no heartbeats to count and no voice to speak.

And late night when I think of writing all those things you taught me about love,
All I am left with is a book never touched and a pen with no ink,
And I cry deep inside with the death of my emotions emraced with silence,

Don't do this to me,
Beacuse before it was me sleeping on your lap staring at you when I didn't feel like sleeping,
And the next time it would be when I won't wake up.

So,
Make me hold your finger,
Show me how much you love me,
With tears in your eyes and smile on your face,
Take me to the world where we belong,
Before it gets too late.

Pranav Vibhute

MY LOSS

A silent loss now suffered,
Deep feelings, that no one can see.
From when I knew I was pregnant
My baby was part of me.
Each day I'd touch my tummy,
Spoke to my little one.
Planning out our future,
For a family, full of fun.
You came and went so quickly,
Our life together done,
Your time with me was so short,
But my heart you'd already won.
Your place in my heart and memory,
For my lifetime is now set,
You may have lost your tiny life,
But you will be impossible to forget.
I never heard your heart beat,
I never heard your cries,
But you are now a shining star
Looking down at me, from the sky.

Jennifer Collins

DEREALISATION

Trapped in a strange illusion, born knowing the truth but growing to believe lies,
trapped in a world of confusion, like a constant drumbeat that never changes,
Or a book filled with white blank pages, a mind blocked by blurry cages, an audience watching empty stages.
Sitting in a snowy field when the skies are bright and clear, watching life like it's a movie from birth till death,
The thoughts of going insane are your worst fears, letters, colours, memories are not clear,
The space between dreams and reality are far too near, it never stops, it will never disappear.
A frosty glass window blocks reality, forget the ways and laws of humanity, every object you see makes you over-analyse,
There's no emotion, you've forgotten how to cry, just waiting for it all to end when you die,
Through every hour, day, month and year you will fly.

Georgina Margaret Boxall

ANDROGYNOUS ZONE

six ninety-nine, sir
was unexpected, even though
I stood tall and cropped,
in loose black sweats.
I looked between her false
lashes, deciding to wear lipstick
next time I dashed out for semi-
skimmed and chicken fillets.

It's great
to tower
without heels,
dedicated
to the gym,
even if I
can't do
balconette bras.

But it happened again,
sunbathing on shingle
in a bandeau bikini,
dozing against the crunch
of heavy feet passing
loud enough for me to hear
Look at that skinny bitch . . .
. . . or is it a bloke?

I flipped
a gesture,
kept back
the tears
till I was alone:
maybe I did
have balls
after all?

Juliette Hart

AFRICA

'Twas the darkest night on which I was born
From my mother and father I was torn
An unwanted birth that created a stir
They threw me to the side with the label *'Africa'*

Who were these who were so cruel to me?
That kept me in bondage and in slavery
They told me that I was born to serve
But a life of poverty I did not deserve

I needed to break out and set myself free
And for my happiness I needed to find the key
But just when I did, someone changed the lock
And once again, Africa they did mock

They stripped me of my treasures and earthly possessions
And left me living a life under many oppressions
Having tried before to get out of this life unfair
All hope had fled, in entered despair

Refusing to accept defeat
I struggled back onto my feet
Upon rejection and depression my life I did build
For I realised it was me against the world

Finding my purpose in this world, with all I had planned
While the world was sitting, I took the stand
And because the world saw the potential inside of me
Set out to help me become the best continent I can be

I have learned that when you have faith in yourself, others will too
and soon they will set out to help and push you through
For this purpose, the world is slowly coming together and has made me strongly believe
World peace will no longer be a thoughtful desire, but one finally achieved

Adele Renee Fisher

FIGHT OR FIGHT

Nurse! Argh! Nurse!
Tha' betta come quick!
Ahm feelin' shitty
An' ahm rate sick!

There now
Whats the drama?
Let me see –
You filled your pyjamas!

You're alright –
Now don't you fret.
You're just fine
And not dead yet!

Dunno go n'
Leave me by me sen
Tha'll be back bu'
Tha dunno say when!

Have to see Stomach
In bed eight
Not just you who
Needs Nurse Fate

Dunno leave me
In this dotty bay
Ah ain't bin washed
Sen' t'other day!

Five minutes and
I'll be right back
Half an hour by
The old, ward clock.

Dunno dare draw
That bloodee curtain
Ah'll dee b'hind 'ere
Ah'm rate certin!

Doctor Ditchitt and
Sister Wreckitt
Abandoned patient
'Stumpy' Legitt

Discharged himself to
A Holiday Inn, where
Food and facilities
Weren't quite so grim.

What ails our
Poisoned NHS?
Bludgeoned staff and
Patients – in excess!

Maureen Goodwin

FIGHT OR FLIGHT

Every day it's a battlefield,
With nowhere to hide and nothing to use as a shield
Who is my friend? Who is my foe?
I really do not know
What is the deal? Is this really real?
Is this a game?
If not, then who is to blame?
Too much strife
And loss of life
With no near end,
Lord I plead, intervene,
Your helpers please send
For in this time, there is too much crime and no sense of accountability,
Crime against humanity – death distraction and poverty
Those in power know it's wrong,
But they still let it go on
They simply do not care,
Because they know no one will dare
Stand up and fight,
For they have all the might
Well I have heard enough and it's time to call their bluff
I cannot take this anymore, I am declaring war!

Lydia Gachuhi

THE RECITAL
(With thanks and apologies to Gian Carlo Menotti (1911-2007) and Francis Rizzo)

My sad soul searched in vain for true answers
Brewer sang 'The Spectre' and 'Resignation'
Her voice rose majestically towards the heavens,
My life was heading for a new destination,
My heavy heart thinking of your web of deception,
You, mingling with ladies, giving your glances

But - I no longer really know you
Your face, voice, mind and gesture
Almost all of you evades recollection
You are now to me - a sad fleeting spectre
Whose single smile or glance bedims my smile
I no longer know if it was really you I loved

Because my heart once loved so much, very much
It asks no further recompense
I know that all my questions will be answered by such
Lies, more lies, and another question too
Even now, I almost welcome your half-merciful deceptions
And your cunning glance provokes a smile, but no touch

As love waned, the house fell to mere brick and mortar
Sadness daubed the walls with shades of miserable greys
Cracks of mistrust appeared in the paint
I never thought you'd be the one who betrays
Me, your wife and my transparent total trust,
Now you've another, I suspect you'll support her

At the golden banquet of such illusion
My weary heart, once insatiable, no longer feeds
I once loved you, but did I know you?
(You were gorgeous, and fulfilled my then needs)
Reality and Truth then introduced confusion
Were you really the man with whom I made a vow?

What's so sad is that I'm *not* sad - at your having gone,
In fact, I am glad that you have *finally just* left:
So - there'll be no more words - undermining me
I'll be strong, well and coping - certainly *not* bereft
If you love again - as you surely will - I wish you peace:
(The first words we spoke): the course of love, don't pervert

I've re-done the house and now it's *my* home:
Bright colours: fushias, golds and sparkling rose,
Shades of Pacific, Marrakech and South Africa,
With my treasures around me, I feel content - I suppose.
Family and friends say the house looks quite new:
Warm, full of love - your ghost has now gone.

Mary M Robertson

HERE AND FAR AWAY

Here, now
no war

I can see
far away
quiet, empty eyes
behind the fire

Too much food
now here
wasted

You, far away
skinny in Mum's arms

Can you sing
if at night?

No food
smile is a long way

Look at me more
may wind understand you

Go into your dreams
my tears into stars
blink at you

Zhao Liangmei

THE VOLCANO

Insecurity bubbles within the cauldron of anxiety
Like a volcanic eruption
The lava of bitterness and wrath streams down the path of relationships
Hardening them in its wake
Boulders of fear are projected like missiles
Landing on the soft surface of these who are near and dear
Ashes of anger rain down
With their smoking plumes
And pour their burning embers on those who love them
Leaving bleeding wounds

Insecurity born out of low self esteem
Unable to dream
That they are worthy of love
They push and shove affection back to where it came
Until it is withdrawn
The volcano of insecurity has erupted
Leaving desolated and landscape of relationships
In its wake
And there is no escape.

Stella Agunabor

RETROSPECT

I don't think I've ever looked at life from the right perspective,
It's like art, you've got to look from the right perspective,
Irrespective, I can read between the lines to get the deeper meaning that is suddenly undefined,
But that's the point, because it's funny how life can go full circle and I could still struggle for meaning,
Thinking the only thing I do well is breathing, though it got better as a bitter,
Thought dropped into my mind and I felt the shock of when I realised that I was the publisher and author of my own torture,
Quite self-centred. But it's called my life, why wouldn't it be exactly that, in fact I think the key is that,
To be adaptable to stay afloat,
To live and love life,
So I don't need to live twice.

Jawed Khalifa

BORDERLINE

I could never make you understand
Every day feels like a living hell
As I can feel happy or not so well
When I'm with my boyfriend, I want him to stay and not go
As when he leaves he takes my soul
You get punished for being happy
Then after happy, anger comes
Rages of fire without reason
It feels like you've committed treason
Feeling empty is the worst feeling of all
But I know I need to put a brave face on and stand tall
People will not see how I feel outside my home
Having this is the most painful and loneliest existence imaginable
Every day I look in the mirror
But I do not like who I see in that mirror
When someone calls you names, you shake and tears flow like rivers
As you are so trapped inside
You stand there and feel as if you have died
Flushes of running rivers down your face
As after a while I return to base
People think we are so bad
They have everything which we should have had
But when tomorrow comes again I will try my best
And I will not give it any less
Stand up, be tall and brave
My soul will be free from that darkened cave
We see the world in black and white
As we will stand tall and fight
Emptiness of my soul, I hope to be free
Then my heart will have blood within me
Trying to be happy is the key
When one night I go to bed, and awaken and I am free.

Neil Douglas Tucker

AN EXTRACT FROM THE BREAD AND THE BEER

Listen!
Of grassroots buried beneath the tarmacked roads
And buzzing phosphate lamplights reaching high
That look with lofty ambition heavenwards
To mirror stars that stud the blackened sky;
Of neon signs that slowly pulse and pump
Red electric blood through veining streets;
Of towers tall, armoured hard in glass
Where money men spin numbers into gold,
And lowly cardboard cities, wherein lie
The lost and ghostly, right beneath your feet;
Of trees and tyres, burnt out cars and schools,
Of steel, of dirt, of grass, of brick, of bone
Sing now, O Muse, and let your venturous notes
Rise over street side clamour, where are heard
A million voices in a thousand tongues –
Some whispered water over shim'ring rocks
Others pelted hailstones on frozen earth –
Ascend still further, high above the sea
Of zeroes and ones, broadcasts invisible
That wash across the sky as roaring waves,
And from this lofty vantage, spread your fingers
'Cross telephone wires that string the city streets
and with a purposed hand, strum them so that
a chord reverberate shakes the darkling sky.
So, sing of London, but grant that I may see
With your all-seeing eye beyond the stone
And mortar of the city; grant that I,
Like you, may peer between the cracks; that I
May dig into the dirt beneath and bring
To light the bones – our hidden history.
Fire me with your spirit so I may tell
How once among us stood such ancient men,
Shadowy things that walked the rows of corn;
That hid in bogs and fens with shining eyes
And gleaming teeth; the long-horned gods that stalked
The forests deep where men trod not in moonlight
For fear their souls be snatched and sped away.
This land was peopled once with giants huge,
Being beautiful and terrifying;
We shared it with them as two neighbouring plants,
Conjoined in soil with branches intertwined;
But one may grow more hasty than his mate
And greedy steal the sun and nourishing soil,

Choking the other, which weakly withers – dies.
So it was with Man, who built and grew
Farther and wider, until no land was left
For those Others who, pushed from field and green
And robbed of verdant woods where they could roam,
Were smothered by cities, and one by one
They myth became; then fairy tale; then naught,
Obscured, forgot by disbelieving stone.
So it was with London – a city built
Upon the buried bones of giants felled
By that proud warrior's sword, the mighty Brutus.
He spilt their blood, which subterranean seeped
Through caverns dark and deep where Effra flows.
Forgotten, cold and lifeless, those legends lie
Hidden 'neath the concrete, tombed in soil.
But just as season's turn brings forth the sun
To melt the icy armoured ground of frost
And raise the dormant buds out from the earth
So is our season changing, and there will rise
An ancient god conceived in fields of corn
A man born yearly with the springing crops
Who grew as they did till the harvest where
Willingly he gave his life for Man.
They cut him at the knees, bound him with rope
And dragged his body through the fields to bake
And wither, 'neath the burning midday sun,
Before they flayed him, under mill stones ground him:
Thus he gave his life so they may eat
His flesh in hearty bread; so they may drink
His blood as dark, intoxicating beer;
And wild and drunken they would feast throughout
The winter long and dark and cruel, and they
Would raise a glass in memory of he
Who gave his life for them; aloud they cried
'To John Barleycorn – the better man than I.'
So, Muse, give me my voice flight that I may tell
How came this god John Barleycorn to stand,
After so many years beneath the earth
Amidst the tarmacked streets, the towers glass.
For this, lower you sights towards the ground,
Take my hand and downwards let us speed
Hurtling earthwards with such force it seems
That we must shatter on the paving slabs beneath.
But as we speed towards them, so fold us
Silver-thin so that we slide unhindered
Between the pavement cracks and downward go

Further through the labyrinth of soil
Until the Earth gives way and there we find
Ourselves in tunnels, long and lined with tracks
Where snaking trains run through the shadows dark.
There two men wok and cut the soil with spades,
Heads helmeted, their jackets luminescent,
Their skin is slick and damp from labour's sweat.
Their toil is watched o'er by perpetual dark
As stroke upon stroke they cut and turn the soil
Until one man sinks has spade but he finds
Its path is blocked; again he tries but still
It will not budge, and to his mate he calls
'I've found something.' - 'What is it?' the reply.
'I don't know – something's buried here.
Sure, it must be a fair few feet across.'
'Must be a stone,' his mate replies. 'It's not –
I know a stone when I hit one and this
Is not a stone, it's something else.'
'What?' 'I – Well I don't know but why don't you
help me with it instead of jawing there?'
'Alright, alright – don't get your briefs twisted.
Let's see what marvel you have discovered.
Perhaps it's buried treasure. There is a chance
That long ago some bearded pirate stood –
Eye-patched and cutlassed, parrot-shouldered too –
And ordered all the scurvy dogs, his crew
To bury deep his gold for none to find.
Until here come the two of us and we
Discover it, uncover it and then,
Oh boy, my Jackie, you and I will live
As kings, – or better still as bankers!
With fleets of cars and jumbo jets and suits
Pin stripe silk with silver cufflinks too.
And don't forget the girls! Oh man, the girls!
You know how ladies love a lick of gold.
Just at the rustle of the notes they'll flock
In their hundreds – man, there'll be so many
That you won't know what to do with yourself!
Come on, let's dig and so let us begin
Our life of leisure and of luxury!'
'There's no point being sarky – grab a spade
and help me dig this up.' And so they dig.
They turn the turf and peel away the soil
Until they stand in horror – for they see
A finger: knuckled, bony, red like raw
Meat, or sailor's hands entwined with rope

And blasted by the salt-encrusted wind.
'What the hell is that?' 'Well, what do you think?
It's a finger.' 'I can see that you fool!
I mean what's it doing here?' 'I don't know,
But we should get it dug.' 'Are you joking?
That's a finger, and where there's one of those
There lies a hand, an arm, and all the rest.
I am not touching that – let's call it in!'
And then the finger twitched – or so they thought,
For in that half light, oft the mind will play
Tricks on itself, so that one thing may seem
What it is not and vice-a-versa too.
'It moved!' 'It did not!' 'Yes it did, I swear.
Let's keep on digging.' 'More's the reason not!'
But undeterred by his mate's argument,
The man digs on and on and so he finds,
As prophesised his friend, a hand; an arm.
The more he digs away till there exhumed
Lies the body of a man encased in earth.
Still he lies and quiet as the air
That hangs between the two, their eyes both wide
In fear at what their tools have uncovered.
'D'you think he's dead?' 'Of course he's dead!' 'But look –
how peaceful lain, as if he were asleep.
His eyes are closed like that he merely dreamt
And do you smell that festered stench that should
Go with a rotting body? No, he smells
As fresh as grass; his skin's not cold but warm
And not the rigid chill borne of the grave.
His beard is thick as thickets, lips full red,
Sure this man looks as though he did not die
But hibernate he lay, so he felt not
The earth come over him, nor neither saw
The stone or metal that sprang all around
As shooting buds, which blossomed into London.'
He kneels and leans in close. 'What are you doing?'
His mate enquires. 'I'm listening to see
If there's a pulse or any sign of life.'
So, head to chest he lies and there he finds
No pulse or beat of heart, but something else:
Rumbling deep, diurnal earthly churnings
That ebb and flow like to the groaning tide.
He listens as it grows and builds in noise,
The storm rising from chest up to throat
Till all of a sudden the mouth agapes and comes
A thunder crack, the creaking timber's cry

213

Of ships in dreadful winter storms, those squalls
That tear the North Sea up and rip the waves,
Bombarding vessels with wind and sea and salt.
So deep the voice, and shaking, that the two
Fall back and there they see his eyes awake:
Dark pits, as black as forests' hearts and deep,
Where lost one wanders, desperate, seeking light
So to escape the wild and horrid dark.
So filled with dread the two men are that quick
To their feet they jump and fast they fly
Down the tunnels, the ground untouched by toes,
Their cries of terror echoing around
Until vanished they are and silence falls
Again upon the tunnel, dark, empty
Save for the buried man found 'midst the dirt.
Alone, his arms reach out unto the sides
And with colossal effort pulls himself
Out from the earth and up to his full height
An takes a step on his unsteady legs,
Sluggish as a stage whose side is pierced
By hunter's arrow, whose heart is weary
From the chase of dogging horse and hound.
His muscles are wood, knotted like tree roots,
Frozen hard by winter, stiff with old age
But step after step he drags his stumbling frame
From the depths of darkness to the light,
Like a budding shoot that navigates
The twisting corridors of earth upwards
To break its earthly bondage towards the sun.
He walks and walks and walks until at last
A thin shaft of light falls upon his skin –
The first morsel of warmth he's felt in years –
And looking upwards sees there is a grate.
He lifts his heavy arms, the metal grips
Slides it sideways and bursts into the light;
But rather than the warming hands of the sun
An basking fields of corn, he finds instead
Noise, heat, confusion, a battlefield of sound
Blistering lights that flash and burn his eyes.
Beneath his feet not fields but concrete grey
Hard as heartless like rhinoceros hide
And as a fly he feels upon the back
Of a behemoth, a city gargantuate
The ground shakes with every step and roar –
A roar! He turns and there a lesser beast
Black with burning eyes and metal teeth.

He leaps aside to avoid its stampede path,
The cab flies by and from lowered window
The honk of horn, a volley of curses.
He wheels and stumbles, strikes something and turns
To find a face unfriendly, granite hard,
'Oi, watch it mate!' it bellows then is gone
Into the throng of people, as many as
A school of silver minnows in a stream.
They flue and slide around him seamlessly
Till drowning he breaks free from the current
And climbs what seems to him the nearest tree,
Striped black and white, metallic cold and topped
With a glowing beacon. From here he sees
The raging rapids of pedestrians.
His broad and brawny hands, gripping the pole,
Turn knuckle white; his eyes grow fearful wide
As if they're trying to swallow the sight
Of these enormous buildings looming round
That burn from inside with electric light.
All around he feels the piercing eyes
Of passers-by, the stranger's marbled gaze –
And jeers are pelted at him from the crowd
'Who's the loony?' Some crazy fucking tramp
I dunno.' 'Oi beardyman – get down!
Oi, Osama, what the fuck you doing?'
His eyes are dark and darting, looking round
At faces jeering, puzzled or just plain cold
Until at last he fixes on a face,
With hair untamed and wild, with beard as thick
As thickets, eyes dark with a fire that –
It's been so long he scarcely recognized
His own face mirrored in reflecting glass.
No bearing now like tall, dignified corn
That proud and upright bristles in the sun
But rather sees a gross and tangled shrub,
Ugly, knotted with confusion.
At this last straw the camel's back is broke,
And from the lamp he tumbles to the floor,
A ringing crash like to a silver birch –
How far it is that mighty men must fall.
Above he looks – a bruised sky threatens rain;
Underneath, the pavement promises less.
So supine lies, till by the scruff rough hands
Haul him to his feet and there he stands,
Barely, between two officers of law
'Been drinking mate?' 'You caused up quite a stir

Just then with your acrobatic display.'
'So – what's your name, mate? Can you hear me?' Sir?
Look ain't you go some better place to go?'
'Just look – he barely knows what's going on.
And smell him – Christ, he proper stinks of beer.'
'Sir, can you her me? Sir – what's your name?'
It's all too much for him; he feels himself
Slipping under heavy waves of sleep;
But just before dark waters swallow him
He shoots a darting hand out at the man
And by his collar pulls the copper close,
And in his ear he whispers now these words
In voice as soft and low as rustling leaves
A name that all but he have now forgot;
'Barleycorn, John Barleycorn am I.'

Tristan Bernays

SOME PEOPLE

Some people say I am crazy
Some people say I am obsessed
Some people ask how and why
Some people will never understand the love I have for you is real
No one will believe the way I really feel
I will never understand why I feel this way
I hope I can find the words to tell you one day

Lisa Murray

DAMAGED GOODS

She stares upon a dusty window,
Years passed by,
without a glimpse or a flicker
this washed out, aging, sad reflection,
standing alone,
nothing to her name but a fallen reputation.

Who was she? Who was this girl? They say
oh dear, you don't want to know her, she went astray . . .
good prospects, they say,
good looks, they say,
good heart, they say,
pure girl, nay nay . . .

Like a freed prisoner, she explored all wrong-doings for a thrilling ride,
opened her heart to a kafir and gave her innocence away to the darker side,
went against the order of her fate,
and relentlessly questioned the integrity of her tribal traits

Some speculate she was . . .
too open-minded,
too courageous
too ambitious,
all the credentials that make our kind of men suspicious . . .

Empty house, unmarried, no children and never really understood,
she used to be known as someone this girl, but now she is just . . .

'Damaged Goods'

Tahara Miah

FORWARD POETRY
INFORMATION

We hope you have enjoyed reading this book - and that you will continue to enjoy it in the coming years.

If you like reading and writing poetry drop us a line, or give us a call, and we'll send you a free information pack.

Alternatively if you would like to order further copies of this book or any of our other titles, then please give us a call or log onto our website at www.forwardpoetry.co.uk.

Forward Poetry Information
Remus House
Coltsfoot Drive
Peterborough
PE2 9BF
(01733) 890099